Brook Trout Forest

by

Kathy Scott

Illustrations by Kim Mellema

Alder Creek Publishing

Printed in The United States of America

Illustrations by Kim Mellema
Cover design by John Crowley,
Original cover photo by Kathy Scott and David Van Burgel
Typesetting and technical design by Daniel Terpstra and John Crowley
Editing advisor, Johanna Oster

10 9 8 7 6 5 4 3 2 1

Scott, Kathy J., 1954-
    Brook Trout Forest / Kathy Scott

    ISBN (Hardcover) 978-0-9657663-5-7

    Copyright 2011
    1. Fly Fishing   2. Maine   3. Fishing rods—design & construction
    4. Labrador   5. Journals, Diaries, and Memoirs

I. Title
799.124

Also by Kathy Scott
    Moose in the Water / Bamboo on the Bench
    Headwaters Fall as Snow
    Changing Planes

for Tom Helgeson
Friend and Mentor

1939 ~ 2010

Acknowledgements

$\mathcal{S}$omewhere, I once read that there are more books written about fly fishing than any other sport. That rings true with me whenever I consider all there is to know about this elusive art and the world around it, or whenever I step back to recognize all of the individuals who have contributed to the collective pool of fly fishing knowledge. I hope that these pages read as a tribute to them, and especially to those who have carried me closer to a richer, fuller life. While it would be impossible to mention every name, many are interwoven in these pages, and a few need special mention here.

As always, David Van Burgel, friend, husband, patient instructor, companion in all adventures, and source of unflagging support, without whom there would be no story.

Ron Barch and Kim Mellema, my partners in publishing and artistry, without whom there would be no book to tell the story, or the wonderful conversations along the way.

Tom Helgeson. I've never dedicated a book to someone before, but a story that celebrates life and learning, that champions stewardship and embraces friendship, reflects the lessons his friendship brought me. No one could write like Tom. He continued to bring people together, and to live whole-heartedly, with passion, good humor, and great courage, as long as he waded bright waters.

Five unique and knowledgeable friends who were gracious in adding their words to mine include Willis Reid, Kelly Galloup, Joe Healy, Duke Welter, and Jerry Kustich. My thanks to each of you, not only for your support, but for the gift of your sage insights, shared across the rodmaking, fly fishing, and conservation spectrum.

Karla Anderson read the early draft, and offered much appreciated thoughts and support. Thanks, also, to Barbara Van Burgel, Carole Barch, Chris Hutchins, Susan Morris, Paul Christman, Robin Reeve, Burton Scott, Susan Scott, Dorothy Van Burgel, Lyn McLachlan, and Archie McLachlan, as well as Lew Beconne, Barid Helgeson, Kathy Helgeson, and Carrie Joy Smith. Somehow, Bob White and our bush pilot Michel slipped from these pages but not from remembrance. Fortunately for all of us, the giving individuals in each of these groups are far too numerous to list individually: the Kennebec Valley Chapter of Trout Unlimited, FlyFishinginMaine.com's web community, the Maine Council of the Atlantic Salmon Federation, the Three Rivers Lodge, and Lawrence Junior High School.

Thank you, Bob Dionne and Michael Jones, for the memorable fall fishing.

Who better than a fly fisher would understand the ripple effect?

~Wayne Farrington
Educator

September 30th

*A*utumn stirs the heart, the forests of Maine vivid with yellows and reds and blazes of brilliant orange leaves among the deeper greens of balsam fir, white pine, hemlock, and spruce. Brook trout colors. More often than not, they're irresistible. David and I thought we'd just stopped by a fly shop to say hello near the end of September. In retrospect, I'd guess we were scouting September 30th Pool, one of those mysterious and hard to find places we'd fished a few years ago today with a guide from this shop on his day off. Our off-duty friend had done well; David caught a couple small ones, and I was pretty much in over my head at the time. The place, though, was perfect: mossy and moosey, a wild, Canadian border, brook trout stream edged with alders and black spruce. There had been a little snow in the air. Perfect, except nothing even looked at my fly.

We didn't go back again, and not just because the Pool was tough to find, a good hidden hike off a well-branched logging road in the Maine North Woods, but because we'd given our word. As guests, we'd traded its location for a day in the water and our very selective use. His favorite spot, our good fortune to share it, but our obligation not to use the knowledge too freely. "Fish it," he'd said, "with me or when you know I'm not there, but don't

take anyone. Or tell anyone." The angling deal with
the devil. Of course, we agreed, and kept our end
of the bargain by putting the trip out of our minds.

Mostly.

A place like that, it just keeps seeping in.
Beautiful wild place. Lingering appeal.

Then, at the shop, we learned that our friend
had booked the entire weekend on another river.

It's a testimony to how impressed we'd been
on that previous, guided visit, that we could
remember how to find our way back after winding
the labyrinth only once. The North Woods is
notorious for its maze of ever-changing logging
roads, intimate and rugged scenery which seems
unique, but repeats itself over and over. Those
firs, that granite boulder, the two white birch: are
those the landmarks, the place we turn, or those,
up ahead? The mountain ash were bent with heavy
clusters of orange berries, some spilling down to
the gray lichens below in a splash of color. We
continued on, feeling the way, until we found the
place we'd parked.

Two hours later, standing waist deep in water
that measured 50 degrees, but I'd swear was
closer to 32, I was musing over a lot of things in
a cold-induced moment of self-reflection. We'd

located, then navigated moose track trails and North Woods obstacles, boulders and blowdowns, and actually found the stream, and then found the Pool. Being a person who might use beloved, boreal, and brook trout in the same sentence, I slowly realized I'd forgotten how cold and reluctant this brook had been that other September 30th. I'd never seen a rise last time, and I certainly hadn't this time. I had had one subsurface strike, then lost the fly somewhere above and behind me in the alders. I switched flies every few casts until I wasn't sure my fingers would bend any more. No matter. When flurries drift in air scented by spruce and fir, every cast promises excitement, and every snap of a twig might be a moose or a bear, or maybe a lynx.

I decided to work my way back upstream past David, who had also abandoned the Pool for faster water and who assured me that I wasn't the only one freezing and fishless, but having fun. We both moved north, casting our way to the exit landmarks, a log on the bank across from far bank boulders near a pair of dark balsam firs, one with a broken top. We paused to pay our respects to September 30th Pool which had kept us humble. I cast across the center; David cast near the end of the Pool. With untold relief that I wouldn't end the season in this place fishless again, I hooked a six-inch brook trout, wild, native, and uncommonly beautiful in the clear water, white-edged fins suddenly distinct against the dark bottom of the Pool, and I played him in, satisfied. The last day, a border stream brook trout bending the cane rod David had given me, a perfect end.

Then the little brook trout suddenly darted sideways. I felt its weight, stronger now, tugging hard, bending my tip. Not really wanting to tire it too much, I quickly coaxed the little fish closer. The line was coming fast, but the trout wouldn't materialize in the waning light under the overcast until it was nearly close enough to touch. It finally came into sight running straight toward me but turned sideways, odd and unnerving. Then it hurdled away, the line pulling hard into the depth of the Pool leaving almost a wake on the surface. With my trout disappearing into shadow, I started considering that the cold just might be affecting my perception a wee bit. I can normally play a 6-inch brook trout with just the line, and here I was, struggling with the reel and the rod. I raised the tip, and my little trout rushed into view. Right at my feet, it was attacked for a third time by an aggressive, kype-jawed marauder. Suddenly, there was adrenaline everywhere.

"David!" I shouted. "You gotta see this!" The marauder grabbed my little trout, and the two started to roll.

David had time to wade over and witness our struggles. Mine was internal – what could I do? What could I do? I sure hoped I could do something.

Of course, there was nothing to be done. The marauder wouldn't swallow the little trout and be hooked. It wouldn't really tangle up in the line. There was absolutely not a thing to do. We both watched and then went with the inevitable. I relaxed the tension and waved my hand over the battle. The biggest brook trout of my angling life disappeared. I checked the little one for wounds. "You don't know how lucky you are," I told it, as it scurried away, less battered than I'd imagined. I glanced at David.

"I saw it, too," he laughed.

Finding our way out in the dark wasn't as bad as it could have been. Even playing chicken with adolescent moose all along the tote road didn't do much more than keep us alert. There were bamboo rods in the air between us. Living in a split bamboo rod making shop, literally, we tend to think in those terms. I'd been fishing the Payne 97 David had given me, his first rod, a 7-foot 4-weight. I was thinking about the little cane rod I'd just made, my first entirely from bamboo strips to the last coat of varnish, just my size, just the rod for small streams and precious little brook trout, a 3-weight Garrison 193 taper. If I'd been using that, what a tug of war we would have had. David had been fishing his Payne 98, still a small stream rod, our usual choice. But this marauder, we'd estimated his length as approaching two feet; how much he weighed, I had no clue. I had a lot yet to learn about catching big fish, granted, but as for an appropriate rod, well, we both already knew the answer to that one, even if we didn't mention it during that long late drive.

<u>September 30th, a year later, Sunday</u>

*M*y morning to sleep in a bit, thanks to David. He walked the pups at their 6:30 a.m. weekend wake-up time, pulling the child/puppy gate across the bedroom doorway to save me from their enthusiasm. It wasn't long before he was back in, though. The sharp-eyed pups didn't think things were right downslope, towards the grassy meadow and brook. Moose.

A moose is always better than sleeping. This one, I could see, was a nice cow. We four perched on the deck to watch as she grazed her way into view far below, disappeared behind balsam fir, reappeared, disappeared again. David and I shared the binoculars. My turn, I repositioned myself toward the far end of the deck. A sleek, healthy cow, moving north.

David's turn, other end of the deck. "The rack's just small," he observed from his vantage point, "like it's a spikehorn bull."

Spikehorn? A moose? I took the binoculars back to see what exactly that meant, pretty sure it was a cow, anyway. I'd looked carefully. The second moose stepped into sight, proving us both right. He followed the cow into full view. We watched her ignore him, watched him pay close attention to her. He stopped to sniff the ground where she'd paused, then raised his nose high, upper lip in the air, and followed her north. His rack did seem smaller than we'd expect, and his movements conveyed his old age, a little bit stiff and deliberate, but with the life in his step that fall days like this bring out in all of us.

The first white frost came last night, mostly down low, where the moose were. Chilly morning, 37-degrees with the sun just up, and 56 in the house, windows still open. A great day for the work of the season; we'd be hauling firewood from the pile into the woodshed, storing and seasoning it for next year.

Even though September 30th is the last day of fishing in the places we frequent, we were going to pass this year. David wanted to design a device, a tool, for straightening short sections of split bamboo for the fly rod he was making, and I hoped to wrestle through a dilemma at school. September 30th Pool wasn't an option, anyway - occupied and off the table. Besides, as if to grant us both the time we needed, yesterday had offered uncommonly good fishing. Good, but telling.

The Rangeley Lakes are just over the height of the land from us, so we'd decided to run up late and check things out. We really expected to be out of luck. If there were anglers on the stream, we'd grant them their privacy and be home for supper. It was too tempting not to have a look, at least, with frost in the mountains and some rain the night before. If we didn't fish, didn't even rig our rods, all the way down to where we'd run out of time wading two weeks ago, we had a chance to cover good distance, fish near the mouth of the stream, and get back before dark.

The trailhead was miraculously devoid of cars.

We waded right in. The clock wasn't actually ticking, but we could hear it in the back of our minds. It would take some resolve to bypass every good pool all the way to the lake, too many temptations. I managed to make it about half way. A tiny trout rising under an overhanging branch turned out to be four inches long. About 5:15, the river widened, slowed, and swept around an extended gravel bar. We more or less alternate, so it was David's turn at a 'good spot,' here being the bottom of the ripples extending from the deep bend, and I moved upstream. I tied on a Woods Special Mike Holt had made for me at his shop on Friday, taking pity on my admitted lack of knowledge about catching big fish. I'd told him about the marauder trying to swipe my little trout last year. I might have told almost everybody; I was pretty excited.

"Try this," he'd offered. It sounded like a good bet.

I was mostly watching David, though, so I don't even know how the strike happened, let alone how I missed the fish. I cast it quickly again, an orange spot among floating orange leaves. The trout slammed my fly. I called to David, a pronounced bend in my little

3-weight cane. He crossed the gravel bar with the net, but it took me a bit to calm the trout down enough to bring it in. Maniac fish. Just the fish I'd dreamed about when I'd made this little bamboo rod, the Garrison 193 taper. We took plenty of photos and measured him, a twelve-inch predator, no 'little jewel' trout here. Stunning colors, almost intimidating. His teeth drew blood. If he'd been, say, a four wheel drive pick-up, he'd have had flames painted on his sides. He disappeared the second I released him.

David caught its rival on his next cast, equally mean and territorial. Equally aflame.

Five fifteen, pitch dark by six-thirty. We had taken two and a half hours to get that far, so we pulled ourselves away. The footing through granite rocks and boulders in the stream, through the maze of game trails in the long grasses and dense fir of the banks, didn't really give me a chance to second guess my choice of cane rods for the day, though I'm re-thinking now. It felt good to have finished the season on one I had made myself, but a 3-weight? It was just as well to end this way, a defiant 12-inch brook trout. What if its older siblings had come up the stream from Rangeley Lake after all? The 3-weight would have been completely out-matched. I was twice lucky, no doubt; perfect trout, and the perfect rod for it.

David has retired to his bench, where he has a rod in progress for a Colorado angler. Our friend Bill Harms had designed the taper and extended us its use. Since David makes rods to experience the craft and the art of it, and to assure their continuance, he treats each rod he makes and each angler who will have it as individuals. Every step, from splitting the bamboo to the final finish, has his full attention. This rod is to be nodeless, the internal dams which support the growing bamboo every foot or so of its length are cut out, resulting in short cane sections. These he split into carefully labeled handfuls of short splits of cane which might need to be straightened before they are trimmed, scarfed, and spliced together into the longer strips which will make up the rod. As an experiment, he's making a small press, so that when he heats a short strip, he can lay it in a form and lever pressure against it, straightening a bend.

Meanwhile, I'm wrestling with a less tangible problem.

A few years ago, I'd started a fly fishing club at my middle school. One of my students approached me over my library desk, and we conspired to make it happen. The curriculum included an activity period at the time, very middle school, 75 minutes set aside once a week for exploratory learning. I thought offering a fly fishing club might satisfy him, Sean, plus attract a handful of his friends, a natural in a state so outdoor oriented as Maine. Fifty kids signed up; the principal drew a dozen randomly, and I slipped in a couple more, including Sean. The first two runs were ten weeks long, covering everything from storytelling to entomology to fly tying to casting to conservation, with the selfless help of some devoted Trout Unlimited friends. The Kennebec Valley Chapter led the way for the first years, until I felt confident going on alone, or with extra hands as needed (which left them free for good work elsewhere). By the third year, there was an active waiting list, and the activity extended to fifteen weeks. We adopted an old gravel pit as the Kids' Pond; Trout Unlimited stocked it. Two more years, and it was on the State's automatic stocking list, there had been articles in the paper and a national magazine, and people were calling to find out how to set up middle school clubs around the state.

Then I came back to the first day of school one fall to find the activity period had disappeared. I cried. I also fielded a lot of student questions but somehow managed to find the high road. In truth, I couldn't really blame anyone in the end. Just one of those things, collateral damage of a schedule change.

The high road, actually, came in the person of the 8th grade physical education teacher. Mike

McGee is as well known as a varsity basketball coach can get in Maine, more than one gold championship ball in his long career. While he's not an angler himself, Mike knows kids, and he could see what the fly fishing activity had done for some of them. He asked me to integrate casting a fly rod into his program, with an optional fishing trip to the Kids' Pond as a follow-up. My principal liked the idea, as did the kids. Even the non-fishers liked the challenge of learning the equipment, assembling the rods, and casting toward a hula hoop under a basket from the center court line in the gym.

Still, in Maine, traditions die hard.

Even though every 8th grader in the school learns to cast a rod now, and my friend Hutch and I had started a true high school fly fishing club, the middle school kids made their wishes known. This year, on the first day of school, the assistant principal coached the assembled 7th and 8th graders on all the great opportunities offered them in middle school. When he opened for questions, a hand went up.

"Are we going to have a fly fishing club this year?" someone near the back called out.

There was a pause from the podium, then he directed nearly 400 pairs of eyes toward me with a wave of his hand. I could have just let it go, reminding them that everyone would be casting, even fishing, in phys ed. Instead, I asked them who'd be interested, if we did have a club. I thought about seventy-five hands went up. He says one hundred.

So there it is. No time slot, kids interested, and I've already shed tears and moved on once. Do I really want to go there again?

In Jim Harrison's movie, Legends of the Fall, someone asks why this young person should learn new things. The answer is my favorite line of the movie. Colonel Ludlow, somewhat taken back, says, "Why, to live a richer, fuller life, of course."

To live a richer, fuller life.

That's how I think about teaching kids to fly fish. Any kid, anywhere, not just here.

Sure, it'd be nice if they'd save the planet some day. Even just the watery parts of it.

And, yes, maybe one in a thousand will find a career as a professional guide or outfit a fly shop. Maybe one in ten thousand.

But what if one of them simply discovers the peace of matching the late evening hatch and

finding a willing trout? Or starts the day outside
at sunrise pulling a popper through early morning
lily pads? Or finally stalks a secretive legend
to a hidden lair, lost in the anticipation of its
tremendous presence?

One of my students, a junior, had a heart-to-
heart with me the night of our first high school
outing on the river. "I just didn't get it," she said,
"even when you found us waders and boots. I
don't know why, but I had no idea we'd actually be
wading in a river. I never imagined how beautiful it
would be."

I think of teaching kids fly fishing as giving
them the choice, as granting them their right to
decide. Without the chance to try it, the offer, the
option, there is no choice.

"Everyone knows there are rocks in the river.
I knew there were rocks in the river," a seventh
grader had told me. "But who'd have thought that
the fish use the rocks? Places to rest, resting lies,
right? Now I look out at those rocks and I can just
see fish stacked up behind them, like I could see
under water."

A fuller, richer life. Not a bad thing to offer a
kid. Not a bad goal for anyone.

Kathy Scott

October 27th, Saturday

*T*he warmth of the woodstove has almost lulled
me back to sleep. The pups feel it too, Effie
sprawled on the dogbed near the glass doors,
Midge snug in the chair she claimed almost the
first day here after the animal shelter. The two are
beautiful littermates, soft and cuddly, long feathers
of silk draping from their curled tails. Effie, with
a black cape but head and legs highlighted with
patches of brown and just a little white, is named
for F. E. Thomas, who made fly rods using a
browntone process for the finish. Midge, dark like
a pesky blackfly, a midge in Maine, is black and tan.
They both somehow sleep with one eye open to see
if this or that noise is a red squirrel, amusement of
choice. Between them, David is planing, the long,
slow, pleasing slide of metal gliding on bamboo,
curls of cane flowing each time.

Writing letters would be a lost art, at least in
my world, except that our friend Tom Waters
keeps it alive for me. His last came from his cabin,
and the rich detail of his life there with Sara, his
Brittany, explains why it's his place of choice. I
just wrote him two, a surprise to thank him for
his inspiration, one to his home in Minnesota and
one to the cabin. Anyone past eighty deserves two
letters once in a while, especially someone who has
spent sixty of them defending cold waters.

Tom is one of many special people, all anglers and conservation advocates, I've met through another Tom, Tom Helgeson. Although he, too, lives in Minnesota, his words and actions bring together the best of the fly fishing, its sense of community. I'll be joining them for a Midwest look at the world late this winter at Tom's Great Waters Fly Fishing Expos. Always fun, so much to learn. Meanwhile, I shared our news on the handwritten pages.

Earlier this week, David took a long lunch to join the Department of Marine Resources biologists and other volunteers helping release Atlantic salmon into the Sheepscot River, a lower Kennebec tributary with an active run. These were originally from the Sheepscot, reared elsewhere, and now being reintroduced to freedom as spawning adults. They must have had some spunk. David was pretty soggy when he returned to work.

The next day, the biologists injected eggs in the gravels of some upper tributaries. I haven't had a chance to help, but David did last year and may later on as they experiment with green versus eyed eggs, trying to find the greatest viability. There's always more to learn. The concept is simple enough. Fertilized salmon eggs injected directed into the gravels of their traditional natal streams will develop as they would naturally, imprint on those waters, and require less care than the streamside incubator method, where maintaining a water flow and guarding against disease always hover. The biologists carry a backpack motorized pump attached to a long PVC tube, which has a valve. They clear the fine sediments from the gravel by inserting the end of the pipe about ten inches into the streambed and pumping down water. Then, they switch the valve and pour the eggs down the tube into the porous gravel.

Much like the method which utilizes boxes containing eggs, mesh coarse enough for fry to escape but still limit predation of eggs, this is hands-off approach. Hands-off, except that in order to gather data, a method for determining the hatch rate is necessary. That's where we'll come in later this spring. Some data has already shown that there are adaptations needed in the process. Last year, the older, eyed eggs did well, but the green eggs, those fertilized just before the long ride to the stream, didn't produce any fry that could be found. The eggs might be too fragile at that stage for such a long ride. This year the green eggs were fertilized on site.

Instead of playing hooky to help, I followed a school day full of classes with a meeting of the high school fly fishing club, our first meeting of this year. This club formed when one of the students who'd been in the middle school activity came to see me from the adjacent high school. Although just a freshman, Mike was an experienced fly fisher.

"I've been thinking," he led in, obviously plotting, "how great it would be to have an official t-shirt from this high school that said fly fishing on it." The high school has blue and gray shirts for every sport, for band, for the math team, you name it. Tradition and pride had seemingly overlooked the obvious.

As far as I could tell, the only thing to do was to help Mike organize a fly fishing group, his real objective. My friend Hutch taught at the high school, still does, and he was willing to be the co-advisor. We both knew how much easier it would be for him to contact students and talk to administrators from the same building; we were and are good enough friends to play the rest by ear. Instead of jumping through all the hoops official sports require, we opted to become a club. Our stated purpose to the powers-that-be was to help students in a consolidated rural high school, with a population of 800, find like-minded students and connect with adults who could serve as role models in a lifelong sport. That was it. Until things started playing out, we weren't promising anything else.

Mike, Scotty, Alex, and the others from that first year have graduated now, and this year's group looks to be a solid core of twelve: seniors Sam,

Cam, Chase, Dillon, and Jon; juniors Ben, Brian, Dan, and another Chase; freshmen Codey, Ross, and Tyler, the upperclassmen all veterans of the club. They met Hutch and me with plans in mind. This year, they chorused, "Let's go Out West," knowing full well that Hutch and David and I do.

"Great," Hutch said. "You guys just raise the money, and we'll go."

They also know him well enough to realize when he's giving in too easily.

"How about this?" I negotiated. "If you still want to go to Grand Lake Stream for the weekend in the spring, like last year, we'll make sure we have that covered first. There are TU camps in the West, too, don't forget that, so if we can't all go, some of you could apply. Then, if you are still interested, after GLS is set, say, a couple months from now, Mr. Hutchins and I will look into it."

Hutch went on. "Ms. Scott and I would like nothing better than to take you guys Out West, and we don't mind asking for permission and making the arrangements, but we know that last year, between jobs after school, studying, sports, and everything else you do, it was tough coming up with the money and the time for GLS. The school budget gives us nothing, you know that." He paused. "Would you rather go West than fish for the weekend at GLS?"

No one wanted that to happen.

We settled into planning the basics: a raffle, our service projects hosting our community Super Boo event and the clean-up of the Kids' Pond, and our group purchase of fly fishing gear through Mike and Linda's shop. Hutch and I promised to check around and see if the school would even allow an out of state fly fishing trip. We both suspected the kids would find themselves too busy for such an effort; they can rarely juggle their schedules to make meetings and haven't managed to get together to tie flies yet.

The late autumn dawn arrived as I finished my letters, but only as the subdued light this overcast allows. A gentle rain has continued from the night, not so much as to be a problem taking the pups out. David tended the fires while I roused Effie and Midge. It's too enjoyable a morning to miss any part of it.

January 14th, Monday

Snowshoed with the pups at lunchtime, a break outside. They'd watched for squirrels through the deck doors all morning; I'd been making furled fishing leaders for the Expos coming up in Chicago and Minneapolis. Leader after leader. As much

as I enjoy twisting up such a useful little rope,
by noon, we were all ready to get out. Snow days
off school are gifts, not to be squandered. For us,
they're traded, each and every one, for an extended
school year, a day tacked on to the end. Miss a
school day now, add it in June. It's only logical,
then, to embrace a snow day as if it is the first day
of summer vacation, albeit a bit cooler.

The first three inches of soft snow had fallen by
noon, making the pups easy to track. Being cooped
up all morning gave them plenty of energy to leave
me behind. Nice just slogging along, breathtaking
and beautiful with the bright layer of snow draped
over the dark balsam fir boughs, outlining every
beech and oak to its smallest branch, clinging to
every hazelnut twig.

We made our way south along the edge of the
beaver bog, the two of them romping out in the
grasses, me in the trees. I considered leashing them
before the South Pond just in case the ice there
was thin, though it probably wasn't. Still, with last
week's thaw and the rushing water, who knew?

I'd have to catch up with them first or entice
them in my direction.

Before I could devise some strategy to lure them
back, Midge found a spot which demanded barking.
When Effie caught up, she was immediately intent

to her elbows, snow flying. They were just both wagging tails, signaling heads and shoulders buried deep in the hole before I snowshoed over.

I love this spot. We used to leave a canoe here before the beaver dams gave way and the water level receded. We scattered a handful of wild iris seeds on the water, and blue flags have grown here ever since. It's mostly wetland grasses and re-emerging alder brush now. Moose still love it, too. That old bull with the smallish rack lingered here in late summer. We saw him once during the fall rut, but there was a larger, more vigorous bull herding two cows through here after that. They had headed downstream, north, passing just below our decks.

The rest of Effie and Midge emerged to greet me. Midgey barked at the hole from a safe distance. How such a cute, puppy-faced dog could have such a deep bark, I don't know, but I do know my cue. Effie stepped aside; I looked in to see a flat, light brown surface.

"Good job!" I praised them. "What'd you find, Eff? Let me pull it out. It won't get you, Midge."

I helped them free their treasure and held it for them to examine, a smallish moose antler. Not shed, broken off. Did the smaller bull lose a fight? I carried it back to the woodshed, escorted by two very proud pups, energized to tussle and play while I looped a rope though a rafter and suspended the broken antler to dry.

Effie and Midge are sleeping in front of the woodstove now, its warm light dancing highlights across their rich fur. Content that their pack is together, the four of us, all is right with their world. They seem so eager to share life with us, drawing us in with pack behaviors like the flagging tails wagging over their find today. We, of course, can no longer imagine our world without them. We couldn't help it if we wanted to, and, of course, we don't. I wonder if the roots of empathy, of affection, come from pack behaviors, a purer form of relationship, uncluttered. Thousands of years later and there's still that feeling of protectiveness, and maybe, too, of some self-definition. Family, rod makers, fly anglers. Our human packs, such as they are, are important to all of us; we couldn't help that if we wanted to, either, and, of course, we don't.

Darkness and eight inches of heavy snow have fallen, with more snow coming down. David finished another dip of varnish on the butt of the cane rod he's making to send to Colorado, the Bill Harms taper, beautiful, too, in the firelight. He paused instead of wrapping the tips when we heard the rumble. The plow swept past, so David stepped into his warmest clothes and headed back out. Through the window by my leader-making bench, I can watch the plume of white from the six-foot snowblower in the tractor light.

January 16th, Wednesday

While it might seem logical that makers of split bamboo fly rods would have a house full of them, we certainly don't. David's first, a Payne 97 tapered rod that he gave to me, hangs in its sock in the closet near the first rod he finally made for himself, a Payne 98 taper. The little Garrison 193 made by Al Medved, our friend and an exceptional rod maker, hangs near my rod modeled after it, that first one I made for myself. All of them are three to five-weights, small stream rods. There are a few old rods more memorable than fishable that have landed here, too, but they're in cases, and need no immediate attention. We keep a small supply of bowling alley wax on hand, a good reason to pause and spend time with fly rods in winter. Even with only four, it sometimes takes until now, January, to look them over, to wax coat the ones that need it, then to store them in the clothes closet. Some years, we pass on the wax entirely, depending on the rod. Well-varnished cane endures.

Hutch and I had met with the high school kids after school, so they were on my mind. We'd listed the things that would need to be done for SuperBoo on the white board. As a service project, much of the list involved partnering with the web community FlyfishinginMaine.com, FFIM. They provide the anglers and the cane, get the word out, and pitch in at the event where we need help. We offer the gym, set it up for displays and casting, organize the registration of the rods on big posters on the wall, and then arrange the gym foyer for a swap table, videos, food, and Matt's Coffee (our official SuperBoo coffee roasted in a cane and wood fired oven). As our only fundraiser, we design and sell commemorative t-shirts.

This year's SuperBoo not only would fall as usual on the day before the Super Bowl, hence the name, but on February 2nd, Ground Hog Day.

David had suggested we try 'shadow casting' as a
t-shirt theme, and the kids liked it. We put our
heads together and came up with a ground hog in
a Fedora standing on a rock casting, a la Brad Pitt's
character in A River Runs Through It. Even high
school anglers know that movie. No doubt
we could get some design help from Abbott
Meader, a local artist in our Trout Unlimited
chapter. To add value for the Kids' Club, we
talked about having a raffle and maybe whoever
won could have Pitt's stunt double, Jason Borger,
personally sign the shirt, if he was game. What
could it hurt to ask politely?

Our club president, senior Sam Miller, followed
me back to the library, somewhat blown away that
we could just google a potential phone number.
He dialed. Jason Borger answered the phone.
Sam explained our club and the purpose of our
fundraising t-shirt, and they worked it through.
Jason and I would both be at the Great Waters
Expo just after SuperBoo; I would bring the
winning t-shirt along for his signature, then return
it to Maine.

Maybe because I was organizing the rods, or
maybe I was thinking about the great meeting we'd
had with the kids, but Wesley Sanborn was on my
mind. Funny, but with him, the word 'maybe' was
the best I could ever do.

The first time I saw Wesley Sanborn, he appeared near my desk in the back of the library, patiently waiting to be noticed. I was busy with three middle school students. Maybe it was his motionless contrast to their very lively presence, but for some reason I looked up. There he was.

"Are you the fly fishing girl?" he asked politely.

The question made me smile. Normally, standing in the midst of twelve year olds, I wouldn't quite qualify as "a girl." While some women might take offense at anyone, especially a man, calling them a girl, it was easy to see that there was no offense meant. The kind face, the wrinkled smile, the aged hands. In comparison, I was just far younger.

I had, in fact, just started the middle school fly fishing club that year; the newspaper had printed an article with pictures of the kids.

"That would be me," I told him.

He stood straight, proud, but with a slight edge that told me he was nervous. Maybe the school, maybe me. He wore the clothes of a man who had worked all his life, maybe at the local paper mill, but I guessed he was long retired. He was slender and only slightly bent with the burdens of life. In his arms, some offerings.

"I read about your students in the paper," he explained, "and I thought maybe they could use some things for fly fishing. I don't need so much any more."

His eyes sparkled at the words "fly fishing."

He laid the gifts on one of the library tables, an old fiberglass fly rod, a few fly tying items, a beautiful wooden net. I picked up the net.

"This has never been used," I said, thanking him. "Are you sure?"

He waved me off, pleased we could use the gear, and was gone. I must have been reeling a bit from the unexpected visit, or he couldn't have gotten away. I searched in the hall, guessing the wrong direction, then came back to ask at the office for his name. He hadn't checked in.

I didn't see him again until the next year, just about the same time. He suddenly appeared at my elbow.

"Are you busy?" he asked. "I found a few more things for the kids."

I can't say why I was so happy to see him, but I was. He read the words in my eyes.

"I have this rain coat," he said (again, it had never been used), "and a few other things that are a little worn. But maybe the kids will like them".

I was ready.

"They'll put them all to good use," I said, "but I don't just teach my students fly fishing. I like to teach them other important things in life, like saying thank you to good people."

He nodded; I had him there. He let me retrieve a scrap of paper, nothing fancy, no big deal to scare him off, and he carefully wrote out his name and address.

"I'll make sure they write," I assured him in my teacher voice. We conspired to make both their fishing and their manners better.

I had his name in hand. His name, and a post office box. My students did write him; I sent their letters along with a copy of my first book, a thank you from me. Then I asked about him at the next Trout Unlimited meeting since those guys knew everyone in the area who had ever fished. Wesley Sanborn. The name didn't ring any bells.

The next year, I felt him in the room before I looked up to see him coming through the door. I was better prepared.

"Great to see you," I said. I thought he looked thinner. It seemed to take longer for him to cross the library with his armload of treasures. He placed them on the table and turned to leave, but I touched his arm. It was lost in his bulky, old coat, but he must have felt the touch because he turned back.

"I can't tell you how much I appreciate seeing you again and all that you've done for my kids," I said, "and I hope you'll accept this as a small thank you."

He looked at the book in my hand, my second, then smiled and held up one forefinger.

"Wait," he said, adding, "I'll be right back".

I understood that "right back" is a relative term when visits are a year apart, so I wasn't worried when I didn't see him for a few days. I knew he'd return.

I was in the middle of a class when I saw him come slowly through the door and cross the room toward me, something in his arms. I had time to close the thought with my students and open my heart to him.

"I'll take that book if you take this," he said. He laid before me an oil painting entitled Devotion, a hen and drake hooded merganser snuggled together near a lily pad, colors muted, blues and grays and greens. I hugged him. The artist had signed the painting to David and me in a script that said dignity, and it also said, "Wesley Sanborn."

I checked the telephone books, googled, and posted on the fly fishing bulletin boards. No one knew him. His address was a post office box, and I couldn't think of a way to trick the postmaster into telling me more. In truth, I eventually resolved to just let it go for what it was out of honest respect. It seemed like Wesley Sanborn wanted it that way.

The next year, Wesley Sanborn appeared on cue, a little bit disheveled and thinner yet, I thought. His voice almost sounded transparent. I was overjoyed to see him.

This time was different, though.

"I went through the closet," he slowly explained, "and this is all there was. It's not for the kids, though. I want you and your husband to keep it."

I tried to say something, but he waved me off.

"I won't be back," he said. "Good luck with your students. It has been a pleasure to know you."

He just left.

That night, I showed David the handsome leather rod case from Wesley Sanborn. It was old, a hundred years or more, but such rich, thick leather, such sturdy, hand-stitched perfection, that it would endure as long, it seemed, as there was fishing. It would outlast even us. I pictured it safely transporting fly rods up the old Sandy River and Rangeley Railroad to the turn of the century fishing paradise of Rangeley Lakes; I could feel the substantial leather of a hundred years of angling entrusted to our hands. The little brass lock was broken, though, so we were able to pull the heavy leather cap off the case. Inside, with the robust fragrance of old leather and time, there were two aging gray rod tubes, still intact, still safe. Inside those, two bamboo fly rods, dulled a bit with age and use, their cork hand worn. They were old, but they were dignified.

We were shocked. It was too much.

I was determined to find Wesley Sanborn, or to find out more about him, at least. There had to be some explanation. Again, at the next Trout Unlimited meeting, I sat with the older guys, the gentlemen with their coffee at their table, urging them to search their memories for any clue, any clue at all.

"Wesley Sanborn?" Jim Thibodeau finally said, "Hmmm. I think my friend Snapper knows him. Isn't he the one dying of cancer?"

The words hit me hard. I couldn't find my breath to ask him more. I couldn't think.

Lying in bed that night, I felt some small sense in all of it. Wesley Sanborn trusted me to pass his

fishing artifacts on to my students who would put
them to continued good use. The next generation
of anglers, the next guys who would run into each
other on the stream, the next guys who would
share their stories when they were the Old Men
Around the Table with coffee and stories in hand.
And the leather case? Maybe it was that simple.
He had passed it on to us, and we would
safeguard it for him, his journey ahead now
unburdened. Knight-errants. Despite my grief, I
accepted that it was a great honor.

He didn't come by again, not the next year, or
the next, or ever. I did receive a phone call from Jim
Thibodeau, though, not long after that last meeting.

"We were talking it over," Jimmy told me, " and
we decided that it's Omar Sanborn who is dying of
cancer. We don't know any Wesley Sanborn."

January 29th, Tuesday

Raining hard in Michigan, tip of the mitt,
according to our families there, but a blizzard is
raging through the U.P., and Minnesota has a
snowstorm tracking along highway 90, Albert Lea
to Red Wing. I'm keeping an eye on the weather
since I'm flying to the Midwest soon. Nice to

know the patterns. Here, we enjoyed the sun and some melting, but their tricky weather is due in by morning. Hope it's not freezing rain.

Walked the pups late tonight after meeting with John Burrows (Atlantic Salmon Federation) and our biologist friend Paul Christman (Maine Department of Marine Resources). Representing our Trout Unlimited Chapter, we solidified ideas about the Atlantic salmon signs we four are creating through a collaborative grant. Under a new policy, Atlantic salmon returning to the Kennebec River after their years at sea are no longer held back by the Lockwood Dam. With help from the DMR, they're ferried to the upper reaches of a tributary, setting up a great potential to shock and delight any unsuspecting angler who chances upon one, thinking it the biggest brown trout ever to swim in that small stream. Informational signs, we'd thought, would give innocent anglers a heads-up.

Wild Atlantic salmon in the back yard, imagine it! Forest creatures like the brook trout, but now endangered, the greater effort is to set right what had gone awry. Their history in Maine is of discouraging results converted to a myriad of honest and often creative efforts to change the tide; we'd helped with Paul's streamside incubation in the early stages of that restoration project. Largely because of him, we don't have to imagine Atlantic salmon in the back yard. I've actually touched one closed to home.

About six months ago, David and I were enjoying a breezy day with an azure sky, a great way to start the summer. Just a little front went through in the night, dropping enough rain to break the heat, not that it had been all that hot yet, maybe eighty. The pine pollen was gone, too, those yellow ghosts drifting down from the high branches every time a breeze blew or a bird landed. With the windows open, every surface inside had been painted yellow. No problem, really. Quick rain outside, quick scrub inside.

We were sorting through the fishing gear when Paul Christman had called with news of a Lockwood salmon. We arranged to meet and picked up David's sister Barb to go along. She lives just a mile from us, and helped tend the streamside incubators during that experiment. If she isn't directly involved, she welcomes Effie and Midge into her home so we can volunteer longer into the evenings. We'd arrived at the rendezvous just as Paul pulled in.

In the back of his department issued, green 4WD pick-up was a cube-shaped tank with an oxygen cylinder attached. He had lifted the lid gingerly as we climbed up the bumper and on to the tailgate to peek in.

"They jump out," he'd cautioned, excitement in his voice, the voice of experience. "She's hugging the bottom. You get to know these fish. If you move quietly, deliberately, and approach her slowly from behind, she'll be fine."

The depth of his caring had been irresistibly contagious. If any creature could command respect, this Atlantic salmon had captured all of us from the dark bottom of her tank.

We looked in, awed, eyes adjusting as he continued.

"She's twenty-six inches long, ten pounds, and pretty pissed," he grinned. Plenty spunky enough to survive the fast ride from Waterville and on upstream to Madrid.

On the next glide past, at the bottom of the deep end of the tank, she had let him touch her or had nudged his hand, I couldn't tell which.

"May I?" I'd asked, trying to turn my excitement into that deliberation he'd mentioned.

Paul is all about education and information. He said yes.

I imitated his excellent example. Her smooth back brushed the side of my hand.

We had followed his truck up the Sandy River to a small farm nestled in a bend. Paul paused to check in with the pleasant older woman who owned it before leading us back her little road to a campsite near a pool. We explored the site, Paul pointing out the details of deep holding lies. He'd placed another female here the week before, likely one of our streamside project babies returned from the sea four years later. This one, he was guessing, was a stray from the Penobscot River.

Paul had fashioned a boot of sorts from half an innertube, one end sewn shut. He drained the water lower in the tank, then submerged the boot. She swam in willingly, disappearing in its darkness. He lifted her and ran for the river. She was far more reluctant to give up her shelter and had no intention of being pulled out backward. Paul was splashed thoroughly before she took off in a huff for the deepest part of the pool, disappearing again. Not totally, though. She was carrying a transmitter Paul would use to locate her the next day and throughout the summer.

I wonder where she is now.

February 2nd, Saturday

David pronounced the Colorado rod ready on Sunday; I made a silk furled lanyard to secure the ferrule plug. We cast it in the high school gym with Hutch, a tradition with all our rods. With a silk line, the Harms 8-foot 5-weight taper cast wonderfully, short and long. Marshall Wardwell, who will see it soon, said it'd be okay to bring the rod along to SuperBoo before we send it out. It was a hit there today.

Who would guess that 100 anglers would brave the Maine winter to drive to a school gym for an event jointly sponsored with high school kids? Split bamboo rods of all tapers and sizes, nearly one hundred of them, were the center of attention. When we had first started SuperBoo, five years earlier, we modeled it after a day in Livingston, Montana, where Troy Miller and other rodmakers had organized dozens of rods at a rodmakers' gathering. It seemed reasonable that if people so well-acquainted with bamboo still enjoyed casting rods of different tapers, and learning about them, anglers who almost never have a chance to experience cane would enjoy it even more. There's passion in that kind of learning. FFIM-ers actually suggested it; we just knew how it had been done. It was a perfect partnership.

During a brief pause between casting, talking, and examining rods, we announced door prizes and then drew for the autographed t-shirt: Shadow casting, SuperBoo on Ground Hog Day, the chubby angler furry on his boulder and sporting his iconic, movie-inspired hat, fly line dancing high overhead. It came out pretty well. The winner felt the absence of Maine's patriarch rodmaker George Barnes, ill and unable to attend, and passed the prize to him. It's that kind of community.

February 11th, Monday

Chicago O'Hare, Gate F10, has loaded the flight to Charlotte. In about an hour, this gate will load for Philadelphia, then take me home to Portland's Jetport, if the weather out there abates. The winds in Maine right now have canceled or delayed some flights.

I rarely travel without David, reasoning that if we can't both go, it'll probably be more fun at home anyway. The Great Waters Expos are the exception, this one in Chicago and the second, later on, in Minneapolis. Great fly fishing shows, granted, but they're also the only real chance I have to sit down with fly fishing writers and learn from them. Instead of our usual roles, me furling and David talking cane, at these I demonstrate furling leaders, but Tom Helgeson encourages me to organize and moderate a panel which fields any and all questions about writing, or, at least, makes semi-believable attempts to say something worthwhile, or entertaining, or, preferably, both. Admittedly, I have a lot to learn, and this is a great way to do it. The Expos are about a third conservation, too, and have a growing youth-oriented presence. Good stuff.

David is still a part of things, as always. Distance apart doesn't change that.

After a hairy ride to the Portland Jetport, whiteout conditions, he delivered me well before the Thursday morning pre-dawn flight. I negotiated the TSA station and waited at the gate while the snowstorm died down enough for his return trip home and my travel west. I was pretty sure the plane would go, less certain when. It had made it in the night before and was at the gate, a good sign. The cold and wind-driven snow had stymied the cockpit computer, but after three re-starts, and de-icing of the wings, we were on the plane. I peeked around the brown foam on my window to see my luggage loaded below as the flight attendant announced that we'd leave if the second engine started. It did. In Philadelphia, they'd re-booked me for a later connection to Chicago without my even asking.

I like flying, even in winter. It's like a game. Sometimes I get to make key moves, other times I just enjoy watching it play out. If there are views, I'm glued to the window, curious and flying. If not, the hum of the plane lulls me to sleep, or I'm so immersed in reading tales of trout or someone's adventures that I lose total track of time. If the flight is delayed, as this one home just was, again, airports are collections of interesting things, interesting people, plenty to do.

My luggage and I had made it to Chicago together, where a taxi driver explained his favorite goat recipe to me, and I told him how I make venison chili. Cultural exchange. Then I was awed to a complete halt by the palace staircase leading into the hotel. Obviously not in Kansas anymore, I spent the evening learning the lay of the place and joining good friends for dinner and conversation.

Friday morning, I slept in a little, until seven, and even discovered how to work the television embedded in the mirror over the bathroom sink. Then I went exploring to see who'd arrived.

Tom Helgeson, as the owner of the Expos and *Midwest Fly Fishing Magazine*, and his son Baird, a journalist who'd graciously agreed to

help out on the Writers' Panel, had already set
up and were helping everyone else. I have a huge
respect for the effort that goes into providing the
angling community with a show like this, our own
SuperBoo being a mini-version and an amazing
handful. The long rows of booths started filling:
Brad Bohen tying muskie flies, Jeff Kennedy
painting, the National Wildlife Federation
people talking over their divider with the Illinois
Smallmouth Alliance. I made note of Oak Brook
Trout Unlimited, key in the Illinois TU camp
for kids; I'd stop by to talk later. Wendy and
Larry, guides and shop owners from Haywood,
Wisconsin, brought along their driftboat. Coren's,
the cane-friendly shop where rodmaker Ron
Barch would be, was set up around the corner, and
Dean Hansen's trays and trays of aquatic insects
spread out beyond that. Carl Heuter from the
North Branch of the AuSable said hello, and Paul
Eberhart, who'd ridden with Ron, offered to watch
over my furling things for me whenever I had to
be elsewhere, making the Writers' Panel infinitely
easier. I turned another corner to walk past the
next row of booths and almost ran into one of the
Expo's nicest gentlemen, Robin Reeve.

Robin pocketed his cell, glumly, I thought.

"It's my birthday today," he said, "and I've
decided to become an asshole."

It took everything I had not to crack up. Robin? A southern farm boy morphed into a Labrador lodge owner, he's as low key and polite as they come. I'd met him a couple times, though I still had no idea what he did for outside work, if anything. I just knew I liked him from day one. Last year, he'd said that David and I should come to his lodge. I had never paid attention to see which lodge was his, had never really imagined myself finding the means, time, or dog-sitter to consider one, anyway. I'd read about them, though. Labrador lodges. My heart raced just in thinking about them, like Maine gone wilder. I'd followed John Gierach's trout bum adventures, and Maine writer-editor Jim Babb had told us about his trips at our TU meetings, but that's as far as it went.

"I don't think that goal will ever work for you," I assured Robin, "but it's your call."

He laughed and shook it off, whatever it was. Then he said, "Hey, I'm glad to run into to you. You know, someday, you and David will have to come up to the Lodge. I really think you two would like it."

He had me there. Without knowing anything more about it, I knew what he was saying was the truth.

Robin continued, "But I don't want you to feel like you have to. Tell you what, let's meet later, so you can think about it."

It was one of those moments when something is so perfectly clear and obvious it takes on a sudden urgency as if it might slip away, or be bushwhacked by more rational thinking. How could anything be more rational, though, than actually living life? As Robin walked back to his booth, I dug for my phone. I pictured David stoking the morning fire.

"Good morning," he replied, surprised to hear my voice. He hadn't heard anything yet.

"You are so going to not believe this," I told him, moving out into the lobby where we could talk. I was pretty much right. I wanted to go to Labrador this summer? We never plan that far ahead, and we've never even considered a lodge before. He did remember one thing I hadn't noticed.

"Are you talking about the Three Rivers Lodge? Gierach? Babb?"

As soon as he said it, the pieces fell into place, my Expo friend Robin and the Three Rivers Lodge articles we'd read over the years. Small world. It started to feel very comfortable. Karma.

We talked about the trip, about Labrador, about staying in an actual lodge (we'd only visited southern Labrador once, camping), and about bush planes. Bush planes! Never in my life has anything sounded so appealing, the out of reach suddenly close enough to touch. Maybe that's why Robin was a little surprised later when I was about to let it all slip though my fingers again. One look at the size of the brook trout, and I panicked; they were completely out of my league. We once drove a thousand miles to fish for tiny native brook trout along the Blue Ridge. Tiny jewels, not the crown jewels. Robin couldn't guess what was bothering me.

"The black flies you can handle if you're from Maine," he explained. "We're all catch and release, and it's river fishing, not trolling. It's an area half the size of Massachusetts with only 10 anglers for eight weeks." Then he added, "You'd probably want 7 or 8 weight rods."

No pressure, characteristically polite, he was just pointing out what I already knew. My kind of place, the stuff of dreams. But we don't even own a 7 or 8-weight rod. The fish were huge; the rods would be huge. This was huge. Too big for me to wrap myself around all at once. Way too big. "Go!" said my heart, but my mind was spinning. My compromise was that at the Minneapolis Expo, if things fell into place, then David and I would come to Labrador.

It's a bit hard to distinguish whether Tom Helgeson organizes a great fly fishing show or throws a tremendous party with the greater group of people he calls friends, a party with heart, character, and depth of purpose. The rest of the weekend, the band that Tom had hired, Chasin' Steel, the interesting side conversations with good people, the Writers' Panel, all went well. If I could be half as wise as poet Larry Gavin, half as sharp as Baird, or know half of the things that Gary Borger has probably forgotten, I'd still have plenty left to learn from them in Minneapolis. Saturday, I looked up Jason Borger, who is so detail oriented, he'd even brought along a pen he felt would be the best for writing on the winning t-shirt. The community of fly fishers is its own greatest asset. Maybe it was some extended kind of karma, but I shared a cab out here to the airport with a friend of Wendy and Larry's. We discovered that he'd been to Robin's lodge and that it looked like I was going. He'd caught a 7-pound brook trout on an 8-weight rod.

March 27th, Thursday

Spring is subtle this year, subtle but persistent. Despite thirty inches of snow on the ground and cold nights, the eaves are dripping and a top corner of the picnic table has emerged from the snowpack. We snowshoed with the pups after work yesterday, and with the lengthening of the days and the time change, we had enough light to lead them all the way back to the snowmobile trail. By then, we had our jackets off. The trails would have been perfect corn snow for skate skiing; I finally took my snowshoes off, too.

We know a spot near Hampshire Hill where pussywillows decorate a wetland, a short hike down the trail. The snowpack is delaying their emergence, but one little, sun-soaked willow wore the first gray, fuzzy harbingers of the new season. March, nearly April already.

The sun was up still, but low, as we returned across the broad expanse of our former pond. Its golden rays bathed the balsam fir and tall white pines of the shore ahead with warmth, the sky above them the deepest blue of evening. Midge heard something first, and following her gaze, we all saw them against that sky, an approaching V of snow geese, sun-brightened white with dark wings. They surveyed us below, re-assembling as they changed direction, looking for safe shelter for the night. The open eddy on the Kennebec, just north, we guessed. We'd found the first flowing water there last weekend, an ice jam building up downstream as the upper river shook free. Spring.

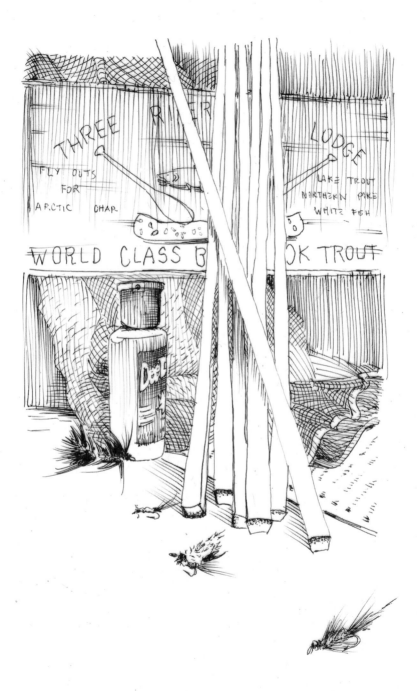

THREE RIVER LODGE

FLY OUTS
FOR
ARCTIC CHAR

LAKE TROUT
NORTHERN PIKE
WHITE FISH

WORLD CLASS B OK TROUT

The weekend ahead promises new beginnings, too. David has finished creating nodeless strips for a rod collaboration. He made joints and glued together splits of small sections of cane sent by Ron Barch from Michigan. He'll send them on to Dennis Higham near Chicago for the next step in the process. In September, a finished rod from several makers' hands will rendezvous with all of us at the Catskill rodmakers' gathering.

So, with David free, we can start anew. On Saturday, we'll pick out the culms of raw cane for two rods. Big rods. At the Great Waters Expo in Minneapolis, I met Robin when we could both slip in a lunch. He showed me a couple blank spots in his roster, places where the camp wasn't full, where they'd be flying, cooking, and guiding for ten but with only eight scheduled. We're going to Labrador.

<u>March 30th, Sunday</u>

Warming, but not too warm, a good day to finish moving the last of the firewood into the basement. We carried armloads in from the winter storage space under the high deck, this year more like a cosy snow cave with our deck floor above it as a roof. The white banks still loom all around, an enclosure about to melt away. Right now, it's hard to believe that there will ever be blackflies, but I'm glad to have the wood moved in before they hit. Blackflies are mentioned twice in the literature from Robin, along with head nets and DEET. Who says there's no place like home?

I reread our packet aloud as David organized his bench. We could each bring fifty pounds of clothes and gear, easy enough. A list included the daily itinerary: coffee at 6 a.m., breakfast at 7 fishing afterwards until supper at 7 p.m.. Then, we'd be welcome to fish the lake for Northern pike or lake trout, or visit with the other guests, or rest. The generator usually shuts down around 10. There was a list of flies. Some parts were amazing: the hot showers in our cabin (we're backpackers, canoe campers), the overnight fly-out to a remote camp, the size of the rods. Robin had recommended 7- or 8-weights, tending toward 9-feet. Our big rods were our 5-weights. We'd been asking some rodmakers for advice.

We had been on the phone with Wes Cooper in Michigan, a friend and wizard when it comes to scarfing a rod, making a short section to repair a broken tip. David rarely does repairs, though he would if it was a rod that he'd made, cradle to grave. But someone we consider a conservation hero had called, Bill Townsend, a rivers' advocate we both admire very much. It may be true that there is no trout or salmon related legislation in

Maine that hasn't felt his good touch; I don't know,
it seems true. He told David that his Art Taylor
salmon rod had been stepped on by a Quebec
guide who felt terrible, and Bill wondered if
David would take a look. Art Taylor lives north of
us in Maine but is the aging artist and rodmaker
responsible for the cover art on the book about
Michigan rodmaker Lyle Dickerson, although
he may be more renown for his breath-taking
paintings of Atlantic salmon scenes. David agreed
to the repair, and called Wes for a consultation. It
was an honor to play a small part in the lives of both
of these men, Bill and Art, and talk to Wes, too.

When we last visited Wes Cooper over the
holidays, we'd started talking bamboo. David
dropped off a different tip, a repair for a friend in
Maine, and Wes finished the scarf in time for us
to pick it up yet that trip. A visit with Wes is like
a gift in itself to anyone interested in cane or in
conservation history. He'd had some interesting
rods in the shop, most notably a Morris Kushner,
one that belonged to Judge John Voelker, aka
author Robert Traver. The Judge's son-in-law, Wes
told us, was seeking some of the much used cane
his father-in-law had fished at Frenchman's Pond,
some Kushners, and an H. L. Leonard or two, and
Wes had repaired them. He also had some other
interesting artifacts in a box on an upper shelf.

Wes showed us a letter from some of his
early Au Sable River friends, asking him if he'd
be interested in a conservation group they were
starting called Trout Unlimited. Wes joined.
Along with the invitational letter, he showed us a
mock-up of the organization's potential magazine,
to be called Trout. In the decades since, his own
local TU Chapter had ebbed into non-existence,
but he was pleased at the growth and endurance
of the whole, the 50th anniversary. Perseverance
is important to Wes when it comes to things he
loves, we could tell: his family, the waters he fishes,
and working with split bamboo. A self-taught
maker, he was approaching 250 rods.

There's a lot to be respected, a lot to be learned,
from people like Wes.

Good to have all the wood in and be able
to move on with the season. Yesterday, I had
transferred the first half of the firewood from the
pile to the basement; then we'd run to Skowhegan
for dog chews, looping back along the Kennebec
River through Madison. We were curious about
that V of snow geese, wondering if they had
landed in the eddy at Old Point and if they were
still there. Snow geese are a rare sight, a good
reason to scout the river and see what's up. Three
pair of Canada geese and assorted ducks, we
decided, but the snowbanks were blocking the

best views from the road. We tried it again early today after our traditional Maine Maple Sunday breakfast, an all you can eat community fundraiser upriver in the tiny settlement of North Anson. The banks were half as high, and the eddy was full of snow geese, on the island, and on the ice hugging the shore. Maybe our V.

This is also the weekend for the traditional sportsmen's show where our Kennebec River chapter of Trout Unlimited teaches fly tying and offers conservation talks. We stopped in last evening and were immediately drafted to take over the Maine Council booth on the main floor. As luck would have it, that placed us right across from an outfitter for caribou hunts in Northern Quebec near Labrador. As the evening grew late and the crowds grew thin, we found some time to chat. He was a wealth of information about the North, the roads, the conditions, the insect myth (he fully believed that anyone living in Maine would be right at home in Labrador). His orientation was more hunting than fishing and a little archeology; he was a flint knapper. His stories about the polar bear made us sad, not that they weren't expected. The only bears the locals see now, he said, were pretty thin, the seal ice being so far out, the bears can't reach them. One more thing we learned. He fishes when he isn't hunting and uses a 6-weight rod, 8 ½ feet long and graphite.

As our discussion continued about which taper to choose for the Labrador rods; Hutch's brother thinks the 8014 Dickerson taper will do all we want. Ron Barch uses Paul Young's Para 15 for bigger fish and water. Wes is with Ron. David asked Scott Chase, a maker-friend here in Maine, who makes lots of Dickersons, but I wasn't sold on the feel when I cast his 8014 at SuperBoo.

"Don't go by mine," Scott laughed. He tends to downplay his impeccable craftsmanship.

I'm no judge and certainly no authority on big rods. My experience with them is near zero and never on the water. It would probably be best to just prepare strips for an 8-foot rod and let David choose.

We finished the afternoon out on the deck in shirtsleeves and ear protectors, perched in sunshine above the snow, working on strips for the TRL (Three Rivers Lodge) rods that we'd split earlier from the culm. The initial steps are the same, pretty much, whatever taper we choose. We ran each of the butt strips and some of the bigger tip strips, squaring the edges. With the beveler and shop vac roaring, we couldn't hear Effie and Midge's bells to keep one eye on them, so we encouraged them to come inside to nap. They trotted right in and were out, tired pups from their squirrel escapades. Afterwards, just as we were cleaning up, we heard the season's first red-winged blackbirds.

Kathy Scott

April 1st, Tuesday

*W*arm and foggy outside; warm with a nice woodstove fire inside.

If the way Robin Reeve is treating us is an indication of the care he gives all of his guests, that birthday resolution just isn't working out for him. He emailed a few more welcome details today: whether we wear our studded boots on the float plane, condition of the road north, other questions he probably gets over and over but answers patiently. We're getting pretty psyched. After work, we stopped by Mike and Linda's fly shop. If you have to work on Opening Day, at least visit a fly shop after work. We probably wouldn't go out so early in the season anyway, but it's still a good rule of thumb. We picked up inflatable belt pack PFD's, just in case the best Labrador trout are hiding in the swiftest Labrador rapids. Extending our range. Or maybe a little nervous; the unknown. Do people wear life jackets while wading?

One of the state's biologists happen to drop by the shop, too. He is heading up to Big Reed Pond tomorrow, trying to find bluebacks, landlocked Arctic char. Illegally stocked bait fish are threatening the bluebacks native to Maine and precious to us. Oquossoc, the native Abenaki called them. There's a small town on the north shore of Rangeley Lake named after them, established back in the days before anglers and well-intentioned but misguided management practices nearly wiped the bluebacks out.

Fresh moose tracks on the trail tonight and some broken shells. As near as we can tell working backward from the clues, signs in the snow, an otter must have found the spoiled eggs we removed when we cleaned the wood duck boxes. One riddle solved. Rotten eggs, that's what Midge rolled in last night. I could hardly rub her with snow, I gagged so hard. When Effie checked out the excitement, her sister rubbed goo across her side, then down my snowpants and finally onto my mittens as I tried to keep them separated. Baths for them both afterwards, so tonight's walk was with leashes. Nice and safe, and fragrance free.

April 2nd, Wednesday

David just clamped the Art Taylor rod in the scarfing block and headed downstairs. He's chiseling it off precisely a few inches down from the ferrule on the broken butt. We both looked it over, trying to pick the best facet for the long cut and chose the side one over from the casting plane. After the piece is removed, he'll measure the cut and match it to the complementary piece he made; then they'll be glued. With any luck, the timing will allow us to bevel the strips we prepped for the twin TRL rods this weekend. We'll make two, both 8014 Guides. The 8014 usually translates to an 8-foot 0-inch rod with a size 14 ferrule, a nickel-silver ferrule with a diameter of 14/64ths. The Guide version uses a 15 ferrule, so the cane there will be a bit beefier. The lore is that Lyle Dickerson beefed up the Guide rods for the Au Sable River guides so that they could pick up all of their line off the water and re-cast it in one stroke. Powerful rods.

There's still no progress toward finding a good time slot for a middle school fly fishing club. Things don't change much mid-year. Since next year doesn't look any better, I decided to test drive the lunch study hall period. Probably being so excited about the TRL trip made me even more sympathetic with the kids. They want a richer, fuller life, right, Colonel Ludlow? Well, at least they want to know where and how to catch fish, the practical side of that idea. Not to mention that the powers-that-be nixed the second potential trip for the high school trip. The first trip, Grand Lake Stream, was secure after SuperBoo, so the kids had asked us to explore a combined fishing and service work option to the Catskills, a little less financially ambitious than a trip Out West, and just as appealing. Word came back that out of state travel is no longer covered by our school insurance.

Obstacles have a way of inspiring action.

The middle school compromise was this: Mike McGee and I worked out a field trip for phys ed. students on a voluntary basis. Since there are Atlantic salmon in the Kennebec River, which flows down from the mountains and passes near the school, we contacted the Craig Brook and Green Lake National Atlantic Salmon Hatcheries between Bangor and Bar Harbor, who welcomed the idea of a visit. Once the school paperwork was completed, I asked any 8th graders who signed up to eat the first lunch with the 7th graders and the entire group to assemble with me during the second lunch.

An interesting crowd. Most of the academically oriented students actually study during the lunch/study hall, or they take an additional class, band or chorus. As these kids arrived, I received a couple of emails from colleagues wishing me luck.

We went over expectations, mostly mine, but they were eager to please. The first three to arrive I already knew pretty well – one has a father who is a fisheries biologist. Next were five friends who sat together but reacted as one; their young ringleader and I were on good terms, so they only required some patience with attempts to be funny, kid stuff. The three girls were strong and independent, a little harder than some but determined to do this

for some reason they weren't sharing. The biggest
kid, I'd been tipped, has a teacher wrathful over a
nasty, page-long letter he wrote about the littlest
here, although the little one doesn't know who
wrote it. I followed up later with their guidance
counselor and the Special Ed people who were
resolving things and assured me the boys were best
friends. They sat together at the meeting. Another
was supposed to be in in-house suspension for
who knows what but has a believer-teacher who
slipped him out for this period. Another one I
know loves to fish but has so irritated his social
studies teacher with his anti-social behavior that
she believes he shouldn't be allowed to go on the
trip no matter what. Twenty kids, twenty stories.

Still, with Mike as their PE teacher and the principals and I all in agreement, if these kids stay good, or serve their time if they're not, they're all going, so, after expectations, we talked about Atlantic salmon being related to landlocked salmon, looked at posters of their life stages, egg to adult, and the migration route. We talked about the Kennebec, how it used to be full of salmon and why it isn't now, the research and experiments looking toward restoration (briefly, getting a bit deep), how smolt traveling out to sea hide under alewives coming upstream, and then what we'd do at the hatcheries. Yes, they could bring pillows, food, cell phones, and iPods on the bus; they'd stay safely on the bus while we're at the hatcheries, but it is a two hour ride each way. Apparently none of them had crossed the beautiful new Penobscot Narrows Bridge, so I made a note to go the long way and to see if we could take them up to the observatory in the highest support.

I gave them a word scramble sheet for the trip. If they found all the Atlantic salmon related words in the list at the bottom, it was worth a free hot fudge sundae when we stopped for lunch. As far as I can tell from their other teachers, most of the kids had it completed before the end of the day.

April 5th, Saturday

*D*avid printed out the numbers for a Dickerson
8014 Guide, a symbolic acceptance of the taper.
He used the measurements from Jack Howell's
book, taken without varnish. We spent the morning
beveling enough strips for two rods into long, slender,
equilateral triangles. A cloudy, 34-degree day, a gentle
fire in the woodstove, a pair of napping pups, and a
little rod work go well. On breaks, the pups mined
the snow and sunflower seed shucks under the
birdfeeder for any red squirrels escaping to the stone
wall, still well-buried beneath the snow. Then, we'd
call them back in to stretch and watch us work, David
feeding in the strips, me pulling them out. He made
the decisions; I marked the beveled strips. With care
and luck, we'll easily have two rods ready for the trip.

Care, luck, and time.

We have an Atlantic Salmon Federation
meeting this coming weekend, the Trout
Unlimited banquet the next. Kids' clubs, salmon
monitoring, preparation for teaching the Catskill
rodmaking class in June. In early July, we hoped
to visit with family and still be back in Maine to
drive North on the 20th. Piece of cake, we laughed.
Don't all good things land on top of one another?

"Well," David paraphrased, "it's all about using
the time we've been given."

"Like Gandalf said to Frodo?" I laughed.

When we'd finished, I snowshoed the pups north. Snow bridges across the brook are few and far between now. It flows like a wide black ribbon through the drifts, deep and swollen with spring but clear enough to count the gravel pebbles on the bottom. An Atlantic salmon stream. I read this week that they once spawned in even these smallest tributary brooks of the Kennebec if gravels were present.

While we were gone, David scraped the excess glue off the repair interface on Bill's rod, then sanded the cane until it made a seamless fit. We returned in time to discuss where exactly to limit the sanding on the rest of the butt. At the signature, we thought, to best disguise the transition, new varnish to old. I helped him pick a red silk thread which, when varnished, would hopefully match the original color on the other side of Art Taylor's name. He'll wrap the length of the scarf in white silk, which will give it extra strength and become nearly invisible to the eye when varnished. Then, he'll fit the ferrule onto the new cane, mask the ferrule so he can dip the rod up to the interface with the original varnish at the signature wrap, and then dip it a few more times over the week ahead. The repair should be back to Bill next Sunday.

Kathy Scott

<u>April 9th, Wednesday</u>

School was almost over when one of the English teachers called me to come to his room. If I wasn't busy, he said, there was a book report I should see. I headed to the 7ᵗʰ grade wing wondering if our aspiring fly fishers had been up to some mischief. We'd been getting a few calls since we'd made them ours. The teacher had sounded pretty positive, though.

Just inside the door to the classroom, a long table was flipped on its side. Brody and Mitch were crouched behind it. Fly fishing kids. The class had prepared the only armchair for me in the part of their circle directly across from the table, now obviously a puppet theater.

Their teacher instructed the boys to begin again, so they introduced their book, Moose in the Water Bamboo on the Bench. Mine. Then Brody showed us his white sock named Kathy. Mitch had one named David but pointed out that he'd be playing the moose, too, and held up the third sock puppet. Brody looked a little less worried than usual, and Mitch, as usual, was unabashed and grinning.

This is how it went:

Kathy: Oh, David, what are you doing?

David: I'm making a fly rod out of bamboo.

Kathy: That's beautiful. Will you show me how?

David: Bamboo is very fragile, so you will have to be careful.

Kathy: You are so smart, will you help me?

David: This is what you do.

Kathy: Like this?

David: That's it. Oh-oh, Kathy, look out for the moose!

(Moose puppet attacks the Kathy puppet, which gets away)

The end.

We all applauded, and I asked them for a copy. Never have I seen such a terrible book report which meant so much!

Kathy Scott

April 20th, Sunday

A hazy sun is stirring a sweet breeze across the deck where I'm taking a break from our tag-team work on the two Three Rivers Lodge rods; we're now calling them the Twins. I really don't want my arm too sore from planing. Breaks are important. Last year I made so many furled leaders with my drill that I couldn't cast half the summer. No sense heading to Labrador the same way.

I'm doing the rougher planing, taking the butts down to nearer their final dimensions. My planing form is set to 20 thousandths over their final measurement, but I'm following a tip from two rodmaking friends, Harry Boyd and Art Port, sliding each strip out the bigger end of the form so I can't possibly over-plane them. David is flattening the enamel side after my step, so he needs some extra to make sure there's enough cane left after that. I hash my cane with felt pen marks, then plane them off uniformly down each non-enamel side, measure to make sure the triangle remains true, that I'm not favoring a side, then do it again. He scrapes the residual char off the enamel side, working it flat with a razor blade. We started before lunch, and I've done all six strips of the first butt. He invested some time setting his planing form precisely and then planed two to final measurements.

The patches of snow are in rapid retreat now. In the woods, there's still more than not, but the clearing is free, except the edges and shadiest places. The entire marsh, the pond and stream area, is snow free, but ringed in white drifts still lingering in the shade under the surrounding fir and spruce. Three mallards floated down the little rapids at the broken beaver dam jetties this morning, feathers lit to iridescent splendor by the spring sun. A wood duck drake came through later, smaller but strikingly beautiful. We watched gray-eyed juncos, black-capped chickadees, and white-throated sparrows share the feeder and the ground under it with a burly little red-breasted nuthatch. A "lbb" hopped into the area and on down the hill, a little brown bird we tried to identify while it inspected the sun-dried ground and hopped off, tail bobbing. Through the binoculars, we found the vivid yellow indicator that we keyed out to be characteristic of palm warblers. They usually winter in Florida then summer here or farther north.

This week's trip to the Craig Brook and Green Lake federal fish hatcheries went well for Mike McGee and me and our lively middle schoolers. If a mutli-week middle school club isn't in the cards or the schedule this year, at least these kids will have a single, memorable day. We crossed the Penobscot Narrows Bridge to a new awareness for them. The volunteer at Craig Brook told us about the life stages of Atlantic salmon in a small auditorium, important and well-intentioned, but I moved to sit strategically between some who grew restless in the hot upper row. Too much like school for them. Not Green Lake, though. After ice cream all around, our bus made the short hop to the second hatchery, and every eye opened wide. They saw rows and rows and rows of tanks and tanks and more circular tanks, all filled with salmon, many covered so their very lively parr wouldn't leap out. We were guided by a biologist who understood young humans very well. He and the entire day were pronounced cool when I spread the trip photographs out in the library afterwards. The kids are already asking about next year. We're all wondering about next year. It will be interesting to see what the next schedule allows.

David is checking a strip to see if a line is a crack, and the pups' bells are jingling just down the hill under the towering white pine in the far corner of the clearing. I looked through the dissecting microscope, using it to magnify the strip while I pinched the cane. The dark line David found closed a bit. A crack. He agreed and retrieved the spare strips for this rod. Of the two squared strips, one was flawed on the pith side, so we chose the other. He'll trim it to match the strip we're discarding while I fetch the pups.

April 22nd, Tuesday

The wood frogs are clucking in a tremendous chorus in the vernal pool, just east, in the dark tonight. Down the hill, to the west, the spring peepers are in enthusiastic chorus, too. The temperature soared to 76 degrees today, but the most stubborn snowbanks linger on. Have to admire them. Most of the ground is bare, though, and heading full steam into spring. A woodcock peented in the bare clearing around sunset.

We worked on the second butt today, sharpening all the plane blades, followed by me roughing and David finalizing.

April 24th, Thursday

Gentle, warm evening, with wood frogs still east, peepers still west, lovely. Work on the Twins continues. David is finishing the last strip of the first tip. I planed all six to the final size of the butt strips, more or less, but certainly equilaterally, and he's done the rest, smoothing the enamel and the final planing. The glue is still too soft to remove from the two glued butts now hanging in the doorway.

David is alternating planes as he works and finishes with a razor blade. I'm using just my low angle Lie-Nielsen plane and will need to sharpen the blade before starting the last six strips, the second tip. Although the trip isn't until the end of July, there is a certain underlying sense of urgency we've tried to waylay with some laid-back persistence. We know how busy things are in May and June: the trip with the high school kids, tending the Atlantic salmon fry traps at the artificial redds, the class in the Catskills, so we can avoid that feeling of pressure to finish the rods simply by working on them whenever we can.

Today, it turns out, is a perfect day to work on cane, not the 80-degree heat of yesterday. Eighty is hard to believe in April in Maine; today is sunny, breezy, and 62. We found the first strawberry blossoms this afternoon, a whisper of white on the west slopes, and the maples are dangling red ornament flowers from every twig.

April 25th, Friday

It's chilly but still sunny, so we set up wooden planing forms angled across the outside corners of the deck railing, David northwest, me southwest, and we removed the excess glue from the sides of

the butts. The blanks lie securely in the V despite
the rough, hardened glue, so they're easier to file. Just
to be sure they were ready, David had heated them
for an hour at about 170 degrees. He works more
efficiently on the rock-hard glue, smoothing one
blank to a satin finish relatively quickly. Meanwhile,
I filed the other in two steps, first to nick the heavy
crests of glue, the wrap marks from binding string,
then each facet again, until there were only shadows,
traces of persistent shine. By then, David was free, so
he offered to finish mine, too.

We both worked down to shirtsleeves. Direct
spring sun feels good.

While we worked, the pups sat dwarfed below
the white pines, looking up to stare down squirrels.
Trying. The squirrels are far too patient for that,
or maybe just too cagy. One finally broke ranks
but was down the huge trunk and up another
tree before the pups could break their trance. You
snooze, you lose.

April 26th, Saturday

These spring school vacation days end as they
began, us sitting out on the deck, feet up, listening
to the spring peepers, watching the meadow and
the brook running through it. The breeze murmurs

through the tall pines. Morning bird song gives way to evening songs, still melodic, but with the bass of the barred owl joining in now and then. Who cooks for you? Effie and Midge lie between us, reluctant to give up their vigil for squirrels, but too tired by evening to hold up their heads. Effie supports her chin on the lower board of the deck railing, staring out between the uprights until her eyes drift shut. Midgey lies on her back, curved slightly for balance, one front leg bent, the other straight up in the air.

We planed the last of the tip strips today. My sharpening skills have been honed a bit, so now I'm twice as fast reducing them to the butt dimensions. David finished the precise final passes as I furled leaders; I seem to have a waiting list, which makes me smile. A list for bamboo rods, I'm used to that, but a list for leaders? Linda needed a few for the fly shop, so while we were there we retrieved my new studded wading boots, as well as new reels with spare spools for these twin rods. Wading staffs, too, essential for Labrador, they say, and probably handy before then.

Two toms are gobbling in the distance, south, maybe interested in that flock of hens we saw earlier while on our walk. There's a silver wake, too, in their direction this evening, a beaver swimming upstream to the jetties and disappearing into the dark stillness of the pond.

April 27th, Sunday

*I*f the tips are glued and bound tightly early in the day, their string can be pulled off and re-done before dark. To make sure, we were up prepping them at daylight. Tips being smaller and easier to bend or twist than the butts, I opted not to risk the tricky parts. These Twins are completely free of ego; David and I just work together however things best fit. Being best friends has brought us a long way together. I mixed the glue, sanded the interior apexes of the cane, and brushed it on, my nose about an inch away so I could sight down the shiny strips for dull, glue-free places I may have missed. None. David did the binding while I stood at the ready with paper towels and white vinegar. By 9 a.m., both tips were blanks hanging bound in the doorway, and we were ready to call the pups.

Road trip.

Grey clouds were spitting rain, chilly, perfect for exploring up through the mountains. We'd been hoping to check on the informational salmon signs, so we headed up along the Sandy River toward Rangeley. They were all in place; vandalism just hasn't been an issue, even in such remote settings with such beautiful comparison graphics of Atlantics and brown trout. Paul said everyone local he talked to along the way was very supportive of the restoration project. It shows.

Some snow dusted the height of the land
but not as much as we expected. We stopped
for sandwiches at the grocery store high on the
mountainside overlooking Rangeley Lake then
continued on through that modest outpost town
past Richardson and Umbagog Lakes to Errol,
New Hampshire, an even smaller outpost town.
A friendly but excited store clerk there persuaded
us to wait through his digital camera troubles
to see, finally, fresh photos of his 21-inch brook
trout, hooked by a nymph on the bottom two days
before, then released. Will we need nymphs in
Labrador mid-summer?

Living in Maine, it's too easy to take brook trout
for granted. Someone once wrote that if you pour
cold water on mountains, you'll get brook trout. If
you pour cold water through forests, you get them,
too. Maine is mountains and forest, head to toe,
and brook trout are so much a part of the culture
here, it's a little surprising to step out of my angling
routine and realize all the things I don't know.

Digging thorough Nick Karas's book on brook
trout tonight, I found that the biggest brook trout,
the trout with the right genetics and a good supply
of food, are usually found north of the 50th parallel,
which we'll be crossing. The Three Rivers Lodge
is a bit north of the 54th. According to Karas, the
brook trout there might be ten years old. He writes

that they live in lakes with a shallow shelf and in the rapids of a large river system. Nymphs weren't mentioned directly, but swarms of Hexagenia were. They also eat sculpin, other brook trout, and mice or lemming.

April 30th, Wednesday

I still have so many leaders waiting that David started filing the glue off the bound tips on his own. The hours I should be sleeping, I've spent restless about the positions – really my friends – cut at school. More to come, we hear. By last night, I was exhausted. It rained all day, dawn until midnight, five inches. Even so, we walked the pups; the beauty and power of it was too enticing to miss. But I was just too tired to do much else. David stayed awake into the night, vacuuming up water that somehow found a path down the chimney to the basement floor. After work today, it was David's turn to nap. The dogs and I inspected the floodwaters, the roaring brook, the soggy trails. While we still have a series of ponds where the stream should be, the rain is settling back into the channel a bit. When we first came to steward this land, the stream was a chain of ponds. So interesting to watch the changes with the weather, with the days and years going by.

Robin sent along a guest information request, ranging from next of kin contacts to our beverage order. The Lodge works the latter in as weight and space allow on previous flights. I couldn't see them having to bring in soda on a float plane, somewhat embarrassing. I filled out the form tonight, conferring with David, still removing the glue from the exterior of the tips.

May 4th, Sunday

Back on track with rodwork and good attitude. Raining all day, not too hard, but nice to have both fires going. Made a venison meatloaf and baked potatoes, rainy day food. David used a lathe to turn the ferrule stations on the butts of the Twins to fit the ferrules, and we glued them on. Looking good.

May 6th, Tuesday

Unusually warm day, 76 degrees. Mushrooms, the first false morels, are pushing thorough the carpet of needles under the white pines. More strawberry blossoms and the first tiny white violets are hidden in the dry grass, but the first green shoots of new grass are up, as are the first adder tongues, trout

lilies. Early fog drifted along the brook, down
through its valley, along with some raucous ravens.
The song of sweet, white-throated sparrows
traveled across the jetties with the pups and me.
Before we'd walked the miles to David, parked
around the corner and waiting to drive us back
home, the wind began building moody, summer-
like storm clouds.

Now, from the deck, I can see fingers of rain
touching the ground in the distance. Not here, not
yet, but soon, according to the whispers rushing
through the pines. Soon.

I just wrapped coarse sandpaper on a small
drill rod, then scraped the interior of the male
ferrules to outfit the tips. David had scalloped and
feathered their tabs on Sunday, prepping them so
their thread wraps would transition easily onto the
cane of the rod. So we'd keep the right male with
its mate, already snugged into place, I slipped
some gray yarn in the ferrule package for one tip
and tied another piece to the matching butt. After
I scraped the metal inside rough enough so the
glue and cane would bond, I dipped the ferrules
in acetone, still keeping track of which was which.
It wouldn't really matter, except that the doctored
exteriors of the ferrules could never be exactly the
same, and switching the mates now could result
in too loose a fit. We'd notice, if no one else did.
Meanwhile, David was turning the ends of the tips

to accept my prepped ferrules. We'll glue them on yet this evening.

Down the hill, the spring peeper community is peaking its wild celebration, a crescendo of single voices blended into a sound like piercing sleigh bells, but the gentler clucking of the wood frogs across the road is winding down.

May 10th, Saturday

*B*amboo has some remarkable attributes. Cane rodmaking has some, too. One of my favorites is allowing us a Saturday visit with some friends across the country while never leaving the shop.

With the ferrules all in place and the excess glued sanded off, we stole a few minutes after a movie late last night to dip each ferrule, in turn, into Jeff Fultz's bluing for two two-minute stretches. We both thought the repetition seemed to make them darker than going a straight four. We had met Jeff in Colorado, though he now lives in Arkansas. I also talked to Ron Barch in Michigan, who read me his grip dimensions for an 8014 Dickerson Guide, the taper of these Twins.

We've been doing a little homework while crossing over to finishing. David checked into two different guide spacings on-line, preferring one suggested by Arizona's Mike Shay. He also asked Scott Chase, here in Maine, who tends to make big rods; his spacings and guide sizes were emailed today. We didn't have size 4 in the bronze Snake brand guides, so we made a list of things we might need. I checked the J. D. Wagner website, then called Jeff and Casimira in Ohio, turning the phone over to David after I'd chatted, so he could, too. We didn't forget to place the order, although it was close.

Afterwards, we switched projects briefly, to choosing cane from a bundle originally selected and imported from China to Seattle by Andy Royer, culms we'd brought back from the Sweetgrass shop in Montana when we were visiting Jerry Kustich and Glenn Brackett. We cut some of those sticks in two for the upcoming Catskills' class in New York, where our friend Jim Krul is the Director.

That left just enough time for David and me to mix a solution of spar varnish and walnut alkyd medium oil so we'd be ready to coat our wraps. We poured 10cc's of each in a tiny jar warming in boiling water and set it aside for use later. The idea is that soaking the wraps with this mixture prevents the air bubbles from forming and causing shimmers in the wrap finish. Alan Kube from Colorado and Michigan's Jim Bureau.

May 14th, Wednesday

*N*ot a cloud in the sky outside, which makes the slight cloud over the day - being stuck inside at a meeting - hardly noticeable. Home late to find the leaves bursting out, grass greener than I remember, and those mysterious bushes by the woodshed which I really should key out someday in full, fragrant bloom. The week has already been pretty full, so a moment to regroup before a little rod work seems a very good idea.

We're still talking about Monday night's Trout Unlimited meeting. Biologists Forrest Bonney and Merry Gallagher filled us in on the status of Maine's brook trout. Maine has 67% of the brookies in the East but has only surveyed 20% of its streams. Almost 100% of the research funding for Maine brook trout comes from non-State of Maine sources. Who knows what subsequent State budgets will dictate? Twenty-four biologists cover all of Maine, with ten summer stream surveyors, the latter about twenty-one years old and very lively. One point stuck with us more than some. The culvert law needs to change. As it stands, the Bureau of Environmental

Protection allows replacement of an old, bad (as in hanging) culvert with a simple letter of intent if the situation is kept as it is, another hanging culvert. Plan to rectify the situation to allow fish passage, with an arched culvert, say, then there's a bunch of paperwork. Bonney and Gallagher shared their collective knowledge and insights throughout the evening.

After the meeting, David wrapped both of the butt ferrules in chestnut silk, tipped them in black, then coated them with our oil mixture. The two tip ferrules were wrapped and coated last night. My turn now, to do the grip wraps, but I'll rest my eyes first. I had that long off-site meeting followed by a rush back to school. I arrived just in time to give my unqualified support to Mike McGee, before, during, and after the assembly we'd arranged in our gym. A major national news magazine presented Mike with a plaque awarding him the Most Humanitarian Coach of the Year for his work in school and out, with his team, his students, and a camp for children with disabilities among other things. Might mean no rod work for me tonight, but I wouldn't have missed it.

Yesterday, Mike McGee directed his class out to the football practice field where I paced off six casting lanes, set up orange cones between them, then positioned five hula hoops about thirty feet away. Five, not six. Middle school kids get a kick out of a little found competition. While I rarely include any overt competition in these casting lessons, I don't mind exploiting a little if it emerges naturally and keeps things interesting for the students who like it.

Late last fall, we taught the first half of the eighth grade inside, in the gym, since it was too cold and windy to bundle up, move outside, hold the class, and still make it to the next class in forty-five minutes. Those kids all have the option of asking one of their second semester teachers if they can somehow join us day after tomorrow for actual fishing at the Kids Pond. Some double up and complete their assignments early, a few just plead so passionately it's worth trading one class period for better attention the next day, and others fall in between. With any luck, none fall through the cracks.

But today was all about introducing the second half of the eighth grade to a rod, reel and line, ten to twenty students at a time. For each of six class periods, kids sat on the granite boulders at the edge of the field. All the rods lay nearby, still in their green or burgundy cases. The reels, also in their cases, filled a small duffle next to a cardboard box full of safety glasses. Mike set the stage, reminding them quickly of the wellness curriculum goals and his expectations for their attention and participation. My turn.

"Okay, you guys," I confided to them, "we don't have any time to waste."

I hurried on to emphasize that point.

"In one class period, you're going to learn to pick out and assemble a fly rod, match it to a line on a reel, and cast a fake fly from those cones down the middle line of the practice field to a hula hoop, then put everything away properly in time for your next class. I think you can do it."

I checked their faces. They were in. By now, of course, they'd heard about this from the first semester students or the kids from last year. Or the years before. If anyone had personal misgivings, the fact that Mike believed they could do it won them over.

"You all know more about this than you might even realize," I told them, as I picked up a rod case. "Maybe you know more about this than I realize. Let's do this. Raise your hand if you've ever gone fishing, any kind of fishing, whether you caught one or not."

Every hand went up. In a place like Maine, it's pretty much a given. We're an outdoor, water state. Tradition runs deep.

"Great!" I encouraged them. "Now, who has spin fished?"

Most hands. Some kids don't know what they did. Middle school is like that.

"Okay! Now, who has fly fished or gone with someone who was fly fishing?"

There are always a few hands. If I'm lucky, there's a student in every class who actually knows how. I don't necessarily ask that student to help me teach; depends on the student and what makes him or her comfortable, but a peer who can fly fish is a great model for the other kids.

"Here's the thing. I'm only going to do this once, and then you're going to do it. This gear costs a lot, and you want to know how to handle it. Everyone here will do what I do."

As I continued, I pulled out the rod, then the reel, illustrating my instructions.

"When you spin fish using a lure or even a glob of worms, they're kind of heavy, right? You can easily throw the lure out to the fish, which would be pretty silly if you were just throwing it away, but you are smarter than the fish. You tie a tiny little line to the lure so you can reel it back to you, right? But if the fish is rising up and eating insects on the surface of the water, making those little dimples, it might be eating a mosquito. Could you throw a mosquito over to those hula hoops?"

I pointed with the rod sections, now in my hands. The students didn't think so.

"Well, I know I couldn't. So I'm going to tie a heavy line instead of a tiny line right on to a fly that is tied to look like a mosquito; then I'm going to throw this heavy line over toward the hula hoop, and the mosquito will just go along for the ride. The trouble is, fish are a little smarter than you think. Imagine a tiny mosquito with a heavy line tied to its throat. How's it going to hit the water?"

An imaginative student demonstrates, and the others laugh at his loud gagging sounds.

"That's right, you guys know all this," I went on. "Even a fish knows that a mosquito doesn't splash down onto the water with a big rope tied to it. So, to outsmart the fish, we take another piece of line, this one tapered so it's thick like the line at that end but it gets skinnier and skinnier until, by the time you tie it to the fly, it's soooo tiny, the mosquito can land, puff, on the water, just like a real mosquito does."

By now, the rod and reel were out, my protective glasses on, and I showed them where to find the rod and line weight notations to match to the right gear and how to line the rod sections up and ease them together just so, not tightly.

"Don't twist them; that way you won't accidentally twist bamboo rod ferrules, but we'll talk about that later. Here's why you double the line over when you thread it through these guides – reel seat where the reel sits, grip not handle, guides not eyes, and now you're all going to say fly rod not fishing pole, right?"

They laugh. Maybe. Then they watched me string the rod the wrong way, let go, and the line fall out. Then I tried it again, doubled over, and the line stopped at the first guide. Enough said. With some yarn for a fly, I offered the time-crunched class the easiest lesson I can.

"Hold the rod with the reel down and grip the grip like it's a suitcase handle. Never bend your wrist: the line will fall in a puddle at your feet or some place equally far from the fish. Then, your left hand, for most of you, holds on to the line in case the fish you catch on the first cast tries to swim away across the football field. You don't want that. With the other hand, you're going to toss that heavy line up into the air somewhat behind you, wait until it's all up there, then almost punch your rod tip forward to about there toward the top of the tennis court fence, to bring the line forward, and let the tip drift down until it points directly at the hula hoop. That's where your fly will land, like this." I show them twice, the hula hoops so close that no false casts are required.

"Now, pair up, find a rod, match it to a reel. When you've strung the line, I'll pull it out (and check the set-up), you'll cast your fly into the hula hoop, and then put everything away again, like this." I demonstrated disassembling the rod, even showing them how to separate stuck sections behind their knees and reminded them to throw down a hat to set the butt and reel in if they aren't on grass and don't want to get dirt in their gear.

I took a breath. Not an ideal lesson, but one that fits. Front-loaded and demonstrated all at once.

"Okay. That's it. Your turn. Do it!"

And they always do. I love to watch their faces when that happens.

May 17th, Saturday

*U*p at 6 am. It was chilly and still overcast, but not threatening, so we worked on the rods while watching the weather decide to clear. We needed to round the butts under the reel seats, precision work. David readied the butts for the lathe, masking them with tape so they wouldn't scratch. I'd helped measure and trim them, so my job for the morning would be to create the grips.

Since I'd already sorted the cork rings, selecting those with the least imperfections for these grips, I moved on to determine their necessary inside diameter. I measured the blank just above where the grip would fit, then experimented with some discarded rings until I found a size that seemed the best fit. I showed David, who agreed. 3/8ths. I moved to a window for the best light and drilled the hole in each cork ring, 28 of them for each grip, one extra for a spare. Mounted on a waxed mandril, twenty-seven cork rings, glued and secured under a bit of pressure, make one grip.

I finished just as David was withdrawing the first of the Twins from the tank of varnish, really spar urethane. The first telling, moment of truth.

"How does it look?" I asked him.

He was smiling.

"Not bad." I interpret that as flawless and beautiful.

The second emerged just as nicely, so we did what anyone would do. We headed off fishing. It seemed like nothing could go wrong.

That same adolescent moose was on the roadside near Cottle, one of our Atlantic salmon tribs outfitted with fry traps. The road renovations

slowed us into lots of time to watch the leggy
youngster, and the thirty-foot shoulder gave
it a safe swath for grazing. The threat of rain
disappeared entirely as we drove farther north, also
good. Things started to change as we approached
the river.

At the near end of the tote road cut-off, tree
length logs were piled high for 100 feet on either
side of the main logging road. More were stacked
along the little two-track access, which was never
more than a tiny gravel passageway, but now had
edges cleared back fifteen feet or so, apparently by
the woods crew. Their land, true, but worrisome.
There hadn't been active logging here before.
Loggers could be anglers, and our usually deserted
stream could already be occupied. As we continued
on, gigantic brush piles appeared every mile. All
of the stumps were about two feet high, mown off
like grass. We finally came to some which had been
chipped, and then we were past it all. We breathed
a sigh of resigned relief; at least this part was still
untouched, we thought. Snowbanks even stretched
across the trail in places, not too deep to cross. In
fact, there were truck tracks.

We followed the mile markers, a new addition,
past a drinking pipe inserted in a spring, also
new. As if to assure us that the stream was still
pretty much as we'd last seen it, remote, clear, and

beautiful, the logging bridges where we usually park were broken and washed out from the spring run-off. Good news; we both recovered our mood.

The bridge over the main branch might have supported our truck, only some of the boards were broken and the wooden timbers were in place. The far end of the rail had been snapped off. Must have seen some heavy meltwater. The second little bridge had several broken planks, but the beams also seemed to be intact. Even so, I checked it out. Too much risk, I thought, to gain a parking spot only 200 feet farther ahead.

David turned the truck around and was jockeying it into a snug spot downstream when a pickup approached the bridges from the other side. I worked my way across the planks to talk to the couple inside.

They were gold dredgers.

Not panners, fairly low-key disturbance of the stream bed people. Dredgers, with a motorized dredge. It was brand new, in the back of their brand new, souped up, and somewhat intimidating truck.

"Hi," the guy driving called out, friendly enough. "You fishing? You should have lots of luck. I've been sucking up ten-inch brook trout all day!"

As David joined us, the driver continued. He was quite impressed with the half dozen little gold flecks he showed us in a tiny vial, before his exit told us he'd decided that we were, obviously, wimps, for not driving across the bridge. No bridge, and by that we took nothing, was going to stop him.

There wasn't what I would have called an opportunity for a insightful debate. The entire encounter was so unexpected, we were pretty much speechless. Neither one of us even knew what was legal here or what wasn't. Sucking up brook trout in a dredge all day, say, or, for that matter, anything in the stream bed, caddis larvae.

It was an awkward encounter. Still, there was nothing to do about it but fish. The water was a bit high but not as high as we'd suspected when we saw the snowbanks along the way in. Current not impossible. No blackflies, no pollen. That was nice. We left the dries behind and fished upstream and down. We tried upstream again, with streamers, with nymphs. At least we had a beautiful walk.

Near dark, we started driving out, but not for long or very far. We both inspected the hissing coming from the rear tire. Flat tire on the new truck. Complete darkness was minutes away, and, of course, the flashlights had suddenly disappeared. Had we even put them in our vests this season?

We gave a NASCAR pit crew a run for its money, though, changed the tire just before the pitch dark deadline and drove on until we stopped to appreciate the four moose safely off the broad side of the new blacktop near Cottle and a slightly more adventurous moose seen, fortunately, in plenty of time. Why does the moose cross the road?

We're both too restless to sleep, so I just glued up the second grip while David dipped the first tip in spar urethane. I'll dip the second. Tomorrow, we'll call around and see if we can learn more about mining in stream bed gravels.

May 18th, Sunday

David rounded the apexes of both butt blanks on a lathe to fit the inside diameter of the grips, now glued but unfinished. Then he sanded the long facets of the butts to dip again. I walked the pups through the explosion of pale bluets, white and blue violets, and yellow dandelions that is the clearing. Blueberries are in blossom, the lilacs are almost out. We were both wondering, though. Patched tires, new tires, one extra spare, two? What do we need to drive to Labrador City?

~ 92 ~

The unexpected intrusions into our fishing yesterday have left me feeling eerily vulnerable yet tonight. The logging, the gold dredger, the flat tire. Somehow, if such a safe and familiar place could feel invaded and at risk, I couldn't help feeling a little unnerved about this trip. Odd. We've been farther north, backpacking an Arctic island, and we've biked, hiked, and driven around remote Alaska. It wasn't even our first trip to Labrador; we've driven up its lower east coast from Newfoundland.

So what was it? Just a restless night? Demons at midnight when I should be sleeping?

And why is that marauder brook trout from September 30th on my mind?

May 31st, Saturday

The pauses in the progress on the Twins are so much a part of the same gentle passions in our lives that they seem less like a departure from rod work, more like depth added to it. We're on to small steps now, a necessity of full work days coupled with the minutia of detail work. We spent one evening sanding the tips, one evening trying to find the winding checks (a follow-up phone call to order more), another evening shaping them into a hexagon to slide over the rod but discovering the new winding checks were the wrong size (with a follow-up call for the next size winding checks, now due to arrive on Monday).

On Wednesday, Jon Dolloff and Sam Miller met us after school out here at the single nearby general store, then followed us home. While we liberated Effie and Midge, the guys transferred their waders to our truck and finished pizza meant to tide them through the evening. We promised the dogs that their Aunt Barb would stop by for a better walk shortly, tucking them back into the shop before squeezing our long-legged passengers into the truck's back seat.

Jon and Sam are both seniors, graduating this Friday, and long time members of the school fly fishing clubs. Sam is this year's president who called Jason Borger about our SuperBoo t-shirt. As a follow-up to last year's Colorado Trout Unlimited camp, both were on their honor to complete conservation work when they returned home. Since I first met them in seventh grade, I've known that these are, in fact, honorable young men, so I had no doubt they'd follow through. When they approached me for ideas, I gave them a menu. Tending the artificial Atlantic salmon redds with us was their first choice.

This was our first trip of the season, so the plan was to meet biologist Paul Christman on his way to the streams to get David and me set up. Paul was all smiles and optimism, as usual, though a little sheepish over the new paperwork requirement he had to enforce. We signed the disclaimer without reading it; no big deal. Good, probably, for Sam and Jon to see that end of field work, too. Then, after what I hoped wasn't too much salmon talk for the guys, certainly interesting to us, we followed Paul's green government issue truck north along the back road, up the Sandy River.

We were almost up to Phillips, a tiny hamlet in the mountains where Cornelia "Fly Rod" Crosby lived and grew up to become Maine's first guide, when we pulled on to the James' farm road and then parked between the house and the barn. Brown, white-faced Herefords, some black Angus, and Hereford-Angus crosses were grazing in a small, fenced-in pasture between us and the river. In the adjacent part of the intervale, the James were planting and weeding in a long, immaculate garden, good brown soil well-tilled. She paused to meet us, younger than I'd imagined, friendly, self-confident, one of the capable organic farmers we'd grown to recognize as the backbone of Maine agriculture. Their autumn celebration, the Common Ground Country Fair, is a Maine institution.

Ursa, a joyous, short-legged chocolate lab, walked the five of us across the farm to the new redd site in the Sandy main stream. The Jameses own both sides of the river, and crossed it there on the solid shallow gravel. Just upstream was the net over the redd. Paul showed us the new, better box, gray with a removable partition and a detachable connection between the box and the netting. We watched him open it, knowing that fry were extremely unlikely so early but caught in the contagious, Christman-like hope that remained undaunted when it was, in fact, empty.

After changing out of our waders, Paul showed us on our map where the other sites were, a new one in Perham Stream, a relocation from last year in Oberton, and the same place in Cottle. The traps allow a sampling of the success of the artificial redds so that Paul can better plan where to establish them and under what conditions. It's quite possible that the ultimate restoration of Atlantic salmon depends on learning new things, thinking outside the box. An added benefit is that the technology could also transfer to reestablishing brook trout in streams where the habitat is viable but there aren't spawning adults. A learning experiment with long arms.

Jon and Sam continued with us, and we four tended the fry traps, exploring the mountain valleys

of those three streams until we had a firm idea of
all of them and the travel time required and we'd
captured the guys' efforts in pictures to share with
the Colorado TU Council. Jon would be flying
back out the day after graduation this year; he'd
been asked back to serve as a counselor at the
Colorado camp, a great compliment. Sam had been
asked to be a counselor at the Montana camp, but
they'd changed the camp dates to the middle of the
summer season, and he'd already signed a contract
to work at a local summer camp. Not even Montana
could entice him to go back on his word. Both
would join the rest of our club and their assorted
fathers, Hutch, and me, for the high school club trip
to Grand Lake Stream in two weeks.

Last night, I walked Effie and Midge for a full
hour, exploring every sniff along the path before
David came home. Then we loaded our sampling
equipment and hip boots to complete the redd
run before dark. It was a peaceful, beautiful
evening, very few bugs, white high-bush cranberry,
viburnum in full white bloom, a lasting sunset, the
richness of mountains in early summer. All of our
streams measured eleven degrees Celsius, though,
still too cold for fry.

Long, refreshing rains this morning. We'll wrap
the tips, either David on one blank and me on
the other, or sharing the feet, one of us up, one of

us down. I'm hoping for the first option, the one which keeps my wraps well away from his more practiced wraps.

Since David finished splitting out the tip strips for our upcoming class, I need to plane off any remnants of the nodes on the pith side today, too. We share the preparation work with our students. A few classes back, we decided that there's only so much that will fit painlessly into a perspective rodmaker's first touch with bamboo. Flaming, splitting, and otherwise prepping the butt strips is plenty for learning those first stages of the process without the toil of doing it for the tips, too. We don't mind giving our students a jump start, and, just in case, we take along full length culms for any student who might want to do every step him or herself.

Effie and Midge are sprawled in front of the sliding glass doors to the deck, the light drumming of the rain making them irresistibly drowsy. The sweet little snores come from Effie. Midgey's paws are twitching, dreaming of squirrels or digging holes.

June 5th, Thursday

The silk thread I used to wrap my rod was YLI and considered to be size 00. Our relationship didn't start out well, but we worked out our differences. Pearsall's Naples is about 000. For these rods, David thought it would be fun to try Pearsall's Gossamer 6/0. Six zeroes? He assured me it wasn't really that much finer.

"I'm game," I told him, "whatever you think."

I suspect my eyes were open a little wider than usual, both in reality and metaphorically. I wanted to show that I was eager to try that unnaturally thin thread of torture, too, but I was also very much aware of how tough that would be.

The gossamer was a real bugger. I might have been better off with a real spider thread.

To add to the challenge, David thought we should share each guide. I'd grown quite happy with the vision of his exquisite wraps on one of the Twins and my less than expert wraps a safe distance away on the other, but, why not? I went along with his I'll-do-one-side, you-do-the-other proposal even though it put my efforts in mirror image location only a fraction of an inch away.

We started off well. He wrapped the hard side, the left, and then I slid on to the stool. I removed my glasses, adjusted the light, and picked up the end of the thread. Holding it in place on the facet opposite the guide, I rotated the rod to secure the thread in place and trimmed off the tag end. Very slowly, I wrapped the fine silk, packing it tight, until I could lay a coarser looped thread across the wraps. Then, I rotated the rod to secure the loop in the wraps. I called David over to inspect my efforts before finishing by pulling the loop out under the wraps, the end of my thread with it. If I played my cards right, he'd do that part; I really didn't want to jinx the good effort by messing it up in the last move. We traded places, David holding my work in place. He pronounced it a good wrap, much to my beaming relief and offered to pull out the loop. Then he lost the end of my thread somehow, and I had to start over. Served me right.

No problem. We swapped places again.

The next wrap, nearly done, I paused at the same place and called him over. That's when the trouble started. He was absolutely gracious, but for that wrap and the next five times I tried, I somehow over-wrapped the very first round. Every time, I'd think I'd mastered it but didn't. He'd wrap the hard side; I'd wrap the easy side, discover the overwrap, and then, in the interest of time and

sanity, I'd ask him to go ahead and redo it. We
finally took a snack break and discussed things.
I explained that I was disappointed; I wanted to
have done those wraps, but I needed to watch
him and figure out what I was doing. He offered
to show me and then take his example wrap apart
again until I pointed out the time of day. In the
end, he wrapped, and I conceded defeat.

The rain let up about two, so we called five
hours enough and drove into town to help with
a festival on the Kennebec, celebrating the return
of the sea run fish and sharing the day with the
anglers and conservationists there.

After a good night's sleep, I had yet another
theory explaining why I had kept crossing that first
thread. I was actually pulling the first wrapped
thread under the others too far when I tugged it
tight to trim it. Maybe. Trying too hard. We tested
my theory, and I wrapped my side of all of the rest
of the guides and the tip top with the gossamer
silk. Problem solved. I left the black tipping wraps
to David over the next few evenings, though; I
coated them with our oil mixture to penetrate the
threads and drive out the air bubbles. The winding
checks have arrived from Casimira, and we're ready
to work more on the butts.

Since we brought up the gold dredging issue
with our local Trout Unlimited directors, looking

for information on its impact, they've urged us to investigate. That's pretty much how these volunteer non-government organizations work, as far as I know. Members see a need, introduce it to the greater collective mind and experience of a board of seasoned directors, and, if it merits pursuing, someone volunteers, usually whoever put it on the table.

So, David and I started the next steps for the group, contacting some other NGO's to see if they had any thoughts. Bill Townsend, Maine's foremost river advocate and associated with several of those groups, can be counted on for sound advice and willing hands, should the cause warrant it. After eight decades, he's pretty much a walking record of conservation efforts in this state. An email to brook trout biologist Forest Bonney, whose territory seemed most likely impacted, was forwarded to Merry Gallagher and others in the regular channels. We mentioned the dredging to Rusty Gates in Michigan in the course of a Michigan conservation discussion, and he ran it by experts there.

No one seemed to think going through a motorized dredge would be good for a trout, but it took some digging on such a unique topic to find the laws. Basically, in the unorganized townships, the wilder lands where no centralized authority presides, dredging seemed to boil down to permission from the Land Use Regulation Commission, the forest's landowner, maybe the Department of Conservation. It was pretty fuzzy to a layperson, at best. The same night that Bill wrote to say that the group Maine Rivers thought they'd look into it, too, reports came through of at least two motorized dredges sighted on the main stem of our primary Atlantic salmon tributary, the Sandy River, and we found a chart promoting the gold panning potential of the Sandy, where fry and parr live and dine, on a State of Maine website.

The light spring rains have been offset lately by heavier downpours and even occasional thunder, the rumbling so familiar over Midwest or Western streams, yet so rare and precious here. Then, last evening, it slowed to just dripping outside, the verdant spring giving way to the lush, deeper greens of summer. The pups showed us a baby porcupine hidden and sheltered on a hemlock branch and hinted that there was another, maybe its parent, masked by leaves in the top of an adjacent beech. I stood on the remnants of an aged but enduring granite wall for a closer look at the baby, a 6-inch puffball. So sweet. It covered its eyes with its little front paws, and we all disappeared.

Kathy Scott

June 10th, Tuesday

*A*nother storm is approaching, the rumble of the
thunderheads nearly continuous in the northwest
and widening to directly west from the deck.
Already the sun is masked, giving the first relief
from an unusual pair of 98-degree days. This
leading edge of the cold front is quite welcome.
Awe-inspiring, really. We've been gauging the
storm's slow advance, the building dark clouds
consolidating in a milky sky, the first slight breeze,
the sudden louder voice booming amidst the
rumble. The white-throated sparrows are singing,
still, and the gray tree frogs seem louder as the
gloom descends. Distinct cheek-a-cheek-a-cheek
birds call back and forth across the clearing from
the woods to the north, then south, then north
again. I keyed them out while we decided what to
do – ovenbird, a woods thrush. The Stokes guide
says it's known for being a bit of a ventriloquist
and mimics the call as "teacher-teacher-teacher".
With the kids' Grand Lake Stream coming up in
four days, it made me laugh.

We had thought about going fishing tonight.
Maybe not, with the storm. Instead, we're reading
a letter just arrived from Robin about the Three
Rivers trip. With the price of oil and the devaluation
of the American dollar, the economy reeling, he
regretted passing some of the float plane fuel costs
along, which we found entirely reasonable. He,

of course and as expected, felt bad about it. How difficult to run a remote, wilderness lodge when forces so far away and so complicated have such a dramatic and, for him, unpreventable impact.

After a relapse in my guide wrapping skills, I spent forty-five minutes doing my side of the stripping guide, then turned the rest over to David in a fair trade for the signature wraps later. That would still equal half the wrapping. Meanwhile, I started sorting and labeling rodmaking materials for six, the students in the upcoming class. I organized what we'd need and what they'd need in labeled bins and made lists of all the things we hoped not to forget. Setting up a complete shop, fully stocked for a half dozen new makers, 800 miles away, is a fascinating exercise, a puzzle of sorts. Did we need this last time? What can be shared? What don't we actually need, but we should demonstrate? What will Art bring? Art Port, from Statton Island, is the third in our trio of instructors. We confer remotely, another puzzle piece sliding into place.

We did squeeze in some fishing time three days ago, a cooler evening before the heat began. We chose deeper, downstream pools and released two brook trout each before we heard a truck above us, winding down the mountain. We scrambled through the thick spruce directly up to a vantage point in time to see it pass. It was a different truck from last time, but as it drove past, we saw the back was fully loaded. Another powered gold dredger. Apparently, we weren't dealing with an isolated incident. My thoughts were changing, though. Perspective is everything, especially when the pot of gold is so different. From the initial shock at the first encounter, akin to outright trespass, granted not on our land but on the resource, the fish's land, sort of, and disbelief that someone would suck up brook trout and caddis larvae and the other organisms living in the gravels, I've settled into something a bit more gracious.

Maybe they just didn't know.

It was an easy mindset to adopt; after all, I wanted to know the impact, the law, all things related, and it hadn't been easy for me to find out. From the enthusiasm of the websites promoting dredging's less invasive sibling, gold panning, I took it that Maine has at least a few very active participants. How much of a leap would it be to go the next step, to gold dredging? On the other hand, granted, there was still the outlaw thought, how hard would it be to get caught way back there? Every endeavor has its outlaws. Most people go by the rules or try to change them. We're known for our democratic town meetings, scores of public hearings, and voter-introduced referendums on every ballot. But Maine isn't a place where anyone is used to asking permission for everything. We don't need as many permits as more populated places, space carries more freedoms. If panning is okay, who would think to ask?

Interesting situation.

We stopped by the Lockwood Lift to see how that project was going. They were raising it with one hundred alewives or so inside, no Atlantic salmon, and never any shad. Shad are the agreed upon trigger fish. When the numbers reach a certain level, as measured by the number caught in the lift, the gears are set in motion for upstream passage at the next dam. With the lift on the west side of the mainstream, there were theories that no shad would ever swim that way. Maybe, but the reluctance might just be a characteristic of the fish itself. We weren't surprised to see Jim Thibodeau near the water. A local Trout Unlimited charter member, guide, and longtime volunteer with my kids, he's fished the Kennebec every day of the year. We also weren't surprised to hear that he'd caught three shad near the lift the night before.

Another interesting situation.

I need to email the Catskill museum the breakfast menu for the upcoming class, pack for the Grand Lake Stream trip with the high school kids, finish some details for Trout Unlimited, then plan for the pups travel to Michigan this summer. Barb will watch over them when we're back in Maine and then off to Labrador.

June 14th, Saturday

Scotty Rice had them all in his hand: the deck of cards and a room full of intent teenage boys. The only sound in the Grand Lake Stream cottage was Scotty's hypnotizing voice and the precise snap of each card as he played them, the cards and the boys. At this moment, the only thing that even approached mattering as much as fly fishing was this card trick, and fly fishing mattered a lot.

Scotty was one of the two oldest - in college, actually. He'd been a part of the school fly fishing club since 7th grade when we first met. That made him the sage, the student turned college guy turned chaperone, the old hand. I enjoyed watching him slowly, deftly, drawing them in.

The youngest watched from the flanks, well aware of their good-humored rank in the school and fly fishing hierarchy. I'd shown them the first card trick I'd ever learned earlier in the afternoon. They had been the first to return to camp as the

midday fly fishing grew more difficult, beyond
their skill and patience level. They had each
released a landlocked salmon early, when the
fishing was best, and that was enough for now.
They'd never seen the trick and were completely
fooled. I'd felt a little guilty. In the end, I taught
them how to do it and had them practice a couple
of times; after all, I'm one of their advisors, and
they're the youngest members of the high school
fly fishing club.

Our juniors studied the cards from chairs,
though the least comfortable chairs claimed
just before supper and after they returned from
collectively catching and releasing three or four
nice landlocked salmon, respectable fish caught in
the riffles just below the nearest pool. They were
too cagey to reveal to the seniors or to Scotty that
they didn't have a clue how he was tricking them,
but their faces gave them away.

The seniors had the good chairs, pulled up
close, or, in the case of the two who had released
fish until dark, they sat on the floor right in front
of Scotty. They weren't so easily lured the rest
of the way in. They demanded that he repeat
the trick, certain they could tell sleight of hand
from real magic, overly confident, maybe, from an
unbelievable day on the river.

Scotty snapped the last card into place, then produced the predicted card from his left pant pocket. Fooled them again. He looked at me before beginning once more; I grinned and nodded. We silently agreed that it was safe. Maybe if Hutch had been there, my co-advisor and the real old hand of the trip, the jig would be up. Not these guys, though, at least not yet, although it was pretty obvious that they were enjoying the card trick even before completely understanding it, much like their fishing.

Two tricks later, Hutch came in with Alex, the other college student, also an alumnus of our program. Hutch guides these kids dawn to dark every year. I'm in and out of the river, seeing often to dry land needs, while he makes sure that every young person has a chance for a good catch. The room was so intensely quiet you could have heard a mayfly hatch.

"What are they doing?" Hutch asked our former student, now his fishing partner, as they pulled off their waders. They'd moved down river to the quiet water where the flies are smaller and the salmon bigger, more selective. In the full moonlight, it was a nice evening for the long walk back to camp after dark.

"Card trick," Alex said. "I know this one, though".

June 18th, Wednesday

*W*hat better way to start the last day of school
for the year than to cast the Twins in the gym
with Hutch? We could cast them outside, and
will, but it was this morning or not until fall with
him, and there's rarely a rod that doesn't debut this
way. Before the first bell, David and I stopped by
Hutch's room in the adjacent building to invite
him along; then the three of us continued down
his empty hallway. The lights in the gym were off
but slowly warmed to full light when we tripped
the motion detectors and started stringing up the
rods, one with a 7-weight line, the other the 8-weight.
Hutch insisted we go first. David tried the eight and
smiled. I tried the seven and forced a smile.

"Maybe you should try the eight," David
laughed. We swapped Twins, and I tried it again.
Better. But my smile felt more genuine when I
watched him and then Hutch lay out line in effortless
casts. I had known these bigger rods would take a
time or two in my hands before we adapted to one
another. It seemed more and more true.

That night, lawn-casting, I could feel the
8-weight line working for me. I couldn't wait to try
it on water, but, with the cane class coming up in
two days, I had no choice.

June 30th, Monday

*A*nother road trip, the third Big Ride of a summer promising to be filled with them, and the pups were glad to land in Michigan for a while. We had driven them to the Catskills' cane class a week ago Friday, eight hours, then back this Thursday, eight hours. Taking the pups along, we'd assured that the Twins might as well stay hanging, curing, in Maine. There's never time for us to fish during a class under normal circumstances, though often our students do; we'd rather stay on call for those inclined to plane bamboo late into the evenings.

There must be something genetic that links anglers to dogs, some common way of looking at the world, some shared attitude. What is a fly shop without a dog?

The soon-to-be-rodmakers in the class all welcomed Effie and Midge with open arms and hearts, taking a moment's break to scruff a head, to offer a little praise, or to volunteer some leg-stretching time. Effie and Midge liked their long naps in the midst of activity in the shop followed by a late evening walk to the bridge to watch the rises in the Lee Wulff pool, or, more likely, watch the birds swooping after the hatches.

A week of such intense rodmaking is a rare joy and builds a lasting camaraderie. In some

ways, it's not so different for me than the Grand
Lake Stream trip, both groups of diverse anglers,
but with a common passionate interest drawing
them together to learn more in a special place. It
is precisely that diversity, that offering of such a
variety of perspectives, that synergistically adds
more to each class than simply the sum of all the
participants. Jack's trek to the Mt. Everest base
camp, Norris's abrupt trip from Iraq to Walter
Reed, Larry's organic lifestyle, Joe's conservation
work, and Rick's flintlock rifles brought depth to
the long conversations over the workbenches and
unanticipated insights into cane.

Four days into his first rodmaking experience
with us, comic writer Alan Cross caught his
father's twinkling eyes across their shared bench
and quipped, "You know, Dad, I've been making
bamboo fly rods for thirty years. I measure my life
in ten thousandths."

While they were laughing together, I thought, I
measure mine in moments like these.

The class becomes a week that is a journey we're
always reluctant to end.

Both dogs protested a bit when we reloaded
the truck for Michigan the day after we unpacked
from the class. Midge had to be carried out of
the house and only settled into the trip when we

indulged her by letting her lie between us on the truck's wide console the first hundred miles. We decided to let them sleep the trip away, driving into the night and pulling into the Michigan farm around one in the morning. Twenty hour drive, not exactly a piece of cake, but we quit counting after we'd made the run home one hundred times. Pretty used to it. We grabbed a nap, then spent the day visiting all around and tidying up from six month's absence. When Effie and Midge were walked, satisfied, and asleep for the evening early, we drove to my dad's.

My dad and stepmother Sue live on the land Grandma and Grandpa cleared after the railroads went through in 1921, plus more they've added to it. They ranch Shorthorn-Angus crosses, Tennessee walking horses, and acres and acres of grass, clover, alfalfa, and treefoil hay. Before he mows, the summer breezes bring alive a palette of greens and pinks and purples and yellows, leaves and blossoms over knee high on me, shoulder high on Effie and Midge. They love to run through the cool morning dew or chase up the mid-day bobolinks, a flash of black and white and yellow. Although Dad and Sue own a great deal of undeveloped lakefront in the back pasture, almost a mile away, it was more practical to build a pond nearer the house, barns, and corral, than to move those back to the lake. All my life, my father had wanted to build a pond, and in that long term, made to last, organic way things evolve on the farm, it seemed the most natural thing in the world to pass the first evening home fishing for blue gills and bass from the shore.

We decided to use one of the Twins, plus David's 5-weight made to a Payne 98 taper. We opted for big flies, a Labrador learning curve begging to be climbed as soon as possible. David tied on a Yellow Diver, and I rigged the smaller rod with a Chernobyl Ant. We both connected with spunky blue gills on the first cast, then cast around until we found their huge cousins and an occasional ten-inch largemouth bass. Fun to see how much the fish had grown in the short life span of the pond.

I fished from the dock at the south end, near the little storage shed and picnic table, David from the west shore. We switched rods to give me a chance to try the Twin on the water. I used the 7-weight line and tried to manage something graceful off the end of the dock, straight out for deeper water.

"Try the edge of the weedbed, near the shore," Dad kibitzed from the seat of his ATV.

He was right, of course, but I couldn't prove it for a while. I joked about his good advice while I did everything wrong with the new rod. Finally, though, I shot some decent line out, let the fly start to sink, then thought there was a little nibble when a huge largemouth burst out, totally clearing the water. Dad realized right away that it was chasing the little blue gill I actually had on, which was handsome in its own right, true, but certainly diminished in my mind. David had been watching from the first big splash.

"You bait fishing?" he called over.

"Not on purpose," I laughed, casting again. Dad had just putted off to the house when I switched to a heavy, Labrador-style cone-headed black woolly bugger. It took me a cast or two to gain confidence that I wouldn't hit myself in the forehead on the backcast. Nothing happened for a while but sand hill cranes landing in the fields behind us. When I was bored enough to try wiggling the fly a bit more, experimenting with movements I thought a leech might make, something was interested. The take was very slow. The 7-weight bent as the unknown refused to surface. Let it not be a turtle, I pleaded.

David came out on the dock to watch.

"A walleye?" He knelt down as I pulled it up. "It's a walleye!"

"A walleye on cane," I grinned, "never done that before."

The Twin and I were getting along wonderfully as the evening turned idyllic, cattle grazing on the distant hills toward the lake, horses in the paddock behind us aglow with low evening light, the first star in the east. The lights were on up at the house and the nighthawks called above us before we put the rods away.

Kathy Scott

July 3rd, Thursday

*D*ad wore his jacket down here this morning, cool
still. We're loving this weather trend, but it's a bit
chilly for the two mile drive around the corner to
our place and for raking hay. For anything using
the Ford 4000, actually. I heard him coming in the
distance, as familiar a sound as if it's always been
a part of my life. The 4000 is the oldest of Dad's
tractors, the first blue one I remember him buying
new, back when I was still raking hay for him with
the little red Massey-Ferguson. The Ferguson was
finally retired as his fleet evolved to the big blue
New Hollands, complete with enclosed, climate
controlled cabs and a radio/CD deck, and the old
4000 became the little tractor.

My older brother and I did our parts with
the haying, one of my most cherished memories
and something David and I continued as long as
distance allowed it. Growing up and years beyond,
the 4000 became my ride around and around the
fields following swaths of mown grasses, a long
beautiful windrow of drying hay trailing behind
me. With no cab and only the tractor's purr and
the swish of the hay, it was just me and the caress
of the breeze or the warmth of hot sun, the calls
of crows or songs of bobolinks, a fawn gently
following a doe in the shade near the woods.
I could sometimes see across my windrows to

David mowing the next field; sometimes I heard my dad driving out to start the baling before my field was finished if the weather was particularly warm and dry. When he did, I'd stop for a moment after I had finished, and he'd pause to maybe add some more twine to the bin, and we would talk, immersed in the wonders and lessons of life on a family farm in Michigan's Up North.

I think there's a link between most anglers and their history. What else could have happened in a person's life that makes fly fishing seem so natural, makes it seem like fun?

Here in Michigan on dark summer nights anglers are fumbling with headlamps and huge clumsy flies while listening for the slurp of invisible big browns in the Au Sable. I've heard of people who would opt, instead, for a nice evening in a fine restaurant or even a good night's sleep. My own friends raise their eyebrows at the choices we make. The wilds of Labrador in July instead of the beach? Float planes and black flies? But I think: the boreal forest with its magnificent rapids and legendary brook trout, the potential to see caribou or discover a lemming's home in the reindeer lichen. I can't even make it sound bad if I try.

How do we end up like this?

When I'm here on the farm, I wonder if I owe my unflagging love of the natural world and my interest in fishing as much to the random chance of my birth order as to anything else.

For five and a half years, I was the youngest, and I was the girl. I didn't really notice since my brother and I spent much of our time together with Mom. Dad was important in our lives, but when they divided the farm work and assorted errands, Mom most often ushered us around, and our play was feeding the pet rabbits string beans while she snapped a bowl full or chasing the chickens while she gathered eggs. But, five years later when my little sister and brother were born in rapid succession, the miracle of pure chance suddenly elevated me to being one of the Big Kids, with all of the gender-free privileges the new division of childrearing responsibilities could muster. Until we grew tall enough to reach the clutch, Mom still had all four of us when Dad was on the tractor, but when they could work in a little free time, Mom would gather up the Little Kids, and we Big Kids were off with Dad.

Dad and Grandpa shared a green plywood rowboat with varnished wooden seats and a false floor of slats that were spread so wide apart that I had to be careful, Dad said, or my foot would slip between them into the seep water underneath.

The boat was wide and stable, which was fortunate because the worms in the can my brother and I worked for an hour to dig weren't the only wiggle worms in the boat.

Dad launched the green boat with us aboard into one of the nearby lakes, pushing from the shore with one leg as he stepped into the boat with the other. He took up the oars with us sitting side by side in the back, and we tried hard to be good.

Whether it was a preventative measure or we'd done something to inspire him, I don't remember, but Dad took steps to make sure we'd all get back to shore safely and smiling. At the edge of the deep hole by the white lotus lily pads, he stopped the boat and looked at us, two little pumpkins on the stern seat trying to pick the flowers and itching to catch frogs. He convinced us that we'd have a better chance to catch fish if we split up, so my brother clamored past him to the bow.

That would prevent any eventual poking or puppy-fights.

Then he fashioned a slipknot from a piece of cotton clothesline and slid the loop over my cowboy boot and tugged it securely around my ankle. He had another one for my brother. The two loose ends he tied to the wooden slats at his feet. He put a worm on the hook hanging from a cane pole for each of us, confident that when and if we fell overboard and floated off like little orange corks, he could just reel us in by an ankle. Or so he told us; I suspect our leashes didn't even extend to the gunwale. Then he tied a popper on his silk line, stood up, and cast with his bamboo fly rod along the rim of lily pads.

Our part of Michigan is right about where you'd wear a ring on Michigan's third mittened finger, just north of the knuckles in the heart of small lake country. Our farm is within a mile of four such jewels, so it was no surprise that Mom headed for a lake when it was her turn with the Big Kids. Mom was an incredible swimmer and had worked summers at a variety of Michigan's shorefront girls' camps. She knew all of the aquatic games, and we never suspected that there were people who were afraid of the water. She would encourage us to swim out with her and to swim under water to see the fish and dancing plants. She showed us how to dive without plugging our noses. Mom could also catch a fish and make it fun. She taught us that bluegills would bite a bit of our sandwich bread squeezed on a safety pin attached to a string if it was presented correctly.

We were comfortable on the water and in the water, and Dad extended our range the next step. One of his turns with the Big Kids happen to fall on an evening when the suckers were running in the outlet stream through our pasture. He bundled my brother and me up against the damp night air, and we tagged along across the long field toward the stream. By the time we reached the fence line, I was too tired to go on. Dad knelt down next to me by lantern light, and we considered what to do. It was a beautiful night.

Although the stream was nearer than I realized at that tender age, the grass by the cedar fencepost was long and soft, and we decided that I would curl up right there and wait until they returned. Dad would leave one of the lanterns on the top of the post where I couldn't reach it, so I would have a little light. He asked me to count the things I heard, every sound, so I could tell him later. I snuggled in to my little nest by the cedar post and watched him move on with my brother to the foot of the hill. I could see their shapes outlined in the glow of the warm light, and I could hear the murmur of the stream. One sound. I looked up at the stars and listened. An owl? Two. A woodcock berzeeping, then whirring. Would that be one more sound, or two? Cows, crickets. My bed was so comfortable, and, out there in the darkness, so was I. I counted myself to sleep.

As the Little Kids grew, we were always much older by comparison. Responsibilities shifted

at times, but when we weren't taking care of
our siblings or helping Mom and Dad, we were
trusted to amuse ourselves. We grabbed tiny
jigging poles and our ice skates in the winter and
hurried off to the lake where our friends were
already fishing. In the summer, my parents bought
us casting rods, and we would walk to one of the
lakes and try our luck with the sunfish, which ·
kept us happy and occupied for long afternoons.
I learned to love the long walks as much as the
adventures at the lakeshore and eventually came to
appreciate the connection between them. If there
were grasshoppers on the trail, the fish would eat
grasshoppers. While bluegills and perch never
taxed my entomological skills, the budding lessons
flowered when I picked up my first fly rod.

Thinking it over, it's understandable when
anglers find themselves happy in circumstances
other people might avoid with shrouded nights
blindly fly fishing the Au Sable or a seeming
lifetime preparing for a trip to Labrador. Chance
and opportunity can conspire to alter perception.
Personally, I am thankful every day that I had
parents who trusted me and taught me to be
wonder-eyed and comfortable in or on the water.

July 7th, Monday

The beautiful, cool nights and comfortable days have warmed slightly with a thunderstorm before dawn and scattered light showers today. While the muggy air of summer has tried to move in, the temperature is still quite pleasant. We've been preoccupied with assorted chores, walking Effie and Midge in the parklike fields between, up, and over the new big round bales of hay and visiting with family and friends. The hometown fireworks were, again this year, the best show ever, and it seemed like everybody was there. The spectacle rockets from the fairground, also home of the high school's football field where I used to march in the band on Friday nights under the lights all fall. In the summer, the July Fourth celebration is followed by a non-electric music share-and-play gathering, known by most as the Dulcimer Festival, swelling the population of the area from two to twenty thousand almost overnight. Tom Waters, my Minnesota pen pal, has attended. So had the dulcimer player from the Great Waters Expo's band, Chasin' Steel. Then, in late July or early August, there's the county fair. Generation after generation, with steers and rabbits, produce from the garden, crafts, or a well-trained horse, most of us have taken a turn sharing what we've learned, what we've done.

Kathy Scott

This year, at fair time, we'll be in Labrador.

We've fished Dad and Sue's pond again, twice. No more walleye (our brother-in-law says there's only one in the pond), but some nice blue gills up to eleven inches, and many of the generation of largemouth that are ten to twelve inches long. We're using only the Twins, me usually with an 8-weight line, David with a seven. We're still experimenting with bigger flies since we're quite used to small ones.

Since the drive north from Maine to Labrador City covers some stretches of gravel, which could mean about anything from smooth and groomed to fist-sized rocks and ruts, we located an extra spare tire on a rim and then crossed it off our list. Robin sent along his own list of things we might want to remember: passports and double-checking the hotel reservation for the night before the bush flight. That's been mostly crossed off now, too. I still want to pinch all the barbs on our flies, clear the pictures from the camera, and make some leaders that'll transition nicely from an 8-weight line to a 2X tippet. The practice on the pond gives me a good chance to experiment with leader formulas.

<u>July 12th, Saturday</u>

*W*e've settled into life nestled amidst farm and family, all too aware that the time here is growing short. Since time also elongates with anticipation, we're living in a paradox. It's a bittersweet parting, leaving next week but going on, at last, to Labrador. The only resolution seems to be to return for the final weeks of summer after the trip North. We haven't broken the news to Midgey yet. She might never get back in the truck. Effie is just as happy to ride here and there, a thousand miles at a time.

They're both growing quite accomplished at navigating the hayfields.

With the hay mown and baled, the fields are transformed into a dog's paradise-a park of short grasses, rolling hills laden with the rich aroma of the grazing nightlife. First, Midge, the athlete, mastered leaping up and over the swelled sides of the big round bales to stand mistress of her domain on their board tops. We only had to lift Effie up once before she discovered all the good smells left behind by the red-tailed hawks who live in the surrounding hardwoods or by the marsh hawk, gray with black-tipped wings. Both glide gracefully over these fields surveying for mice, frogs, and small birds, then pause for dinner on

the bale tops. Both dogs have taken the end of the
bale approach once or twice but mostly jump first
to the widest part of the round side, where the
bale starts to curve back, and propel themselves
the rest of the way up. When it's too hot, Effie just
passes on the gymnastics of her sister and lounges,
panting, in the cool grass on the bale's shady side,
waiting for Midge to come down.

After we walked them today, we found
ourselves in the unusual position of being alone,
family and friends all occupied and the weather
pretty much cooperative. We'd had a heavy rain,
so the rivers could be a bit high, but maybe not.
It's Saturday, too, so the water could be crowded.
Should be. Weighing the pros and cons of travel
time, high water potential, likelihood of people,
likelihood of success, we decided to go to the Pere
Marquette system only thirty-seven miles away,
rather than travel to the Au Sable, twice that.
Better to be crowded out closer to home today, we
thought, plus why not explore some new water?
The South Branch of the Au Sable is pretty much
our home river, and we've spent some time on the
North Branch, the Deward tract of the Manistee,
anything small and trouty in the area. The Pere
Marquette, the P.M., has been a classic case of too
close to home.

Baldwin Bait and Tackle doesn't have the panache of a fancy shop, but it isn't quite the hook and bullet place the name might lead someone to believe. That's all superficial, anyway. What counts is that we found exactly what we needed there: good conversation, the right flies, and sound advice. We stopped in to buy licenses and discovered that one of the guys fishes Wes Cooper cane. That led to talk of Wes, what a treasure he is, and how great it is to talk with guys like Wes, to learn from them. Eventually, on their advice, we drove off for the Green Cottage.

On the P.M., the Green Cottage is famous, a put-in for drift boats fishing the catch and release waters this time of year and apparently a mecca of steelhead traffic the seasons we're never here. To our amazement, we had the parking area to ourselves. We paid the three dollar fee, self service, and pulled out our personal rods, my 3-weight, David's 5-weight. We both chose leggy grasshopper stimulators with green bodies, given green oak grasshoppers around, and stood under the oaks on the sand banks to look down on the river and get our bearings. I knew I had to muster some courage, or at least some technique, before Labrador's rapids and big rivers, but, even so, the current seemed a little stronger, the water a little higher than my comfort zone. We followed the narrow sandy path upstream.

The P.M. has amazing gravel, a few runs of sand, and some mysterious deep holes that harbor, we suspect, big browns. The overhanging banks and alder branches probably do, too. We crossed in thigh deep water to position ourselves to drift a fly into the lies, David holding me securely against the current. It was a little discouraging, but I left him there to fish the deep bend and climbed up the other bank to walk to some shallow ripples where I could manage on my own at least. I no more than floated my gaudy fly down through the sparkles than a little rainbow slammed it, leaping and making a major fuss.

I played in all the bright water I could find as we headed upstream. It was great fun to see what was hiding beneath the burbling little waves, but I kept my eye out for those big fish lies and pointed them out to David, who was fishing the deeper places behind me. When the river widened just around a bend, I saw it. The perfect spot. If I was a huge brown, that's exactly where I'd be, a long sweeping outside bend completely sheltered by overhanging alders.

I stayed completely away.

After David fished up to me, we scouted the possibilities. A fine resting lie, but across strong water. Certainly, my little cane rod would defer to his 5-weight. Far better him than me by all accounts. I held my ground while he passed me and fought the current to gain a better angle upstream. It took some real work. He was just at the head of the sharp curve and preparing to backcast when a drift boat floated almost out of the trees and into sight. The angling client cast straight down stream toward the bend, something tremendous snatched the fly, and the terrible bend of his fly rod had him whooping with excitement. David stood close enough to see the big brown in the net.

"Nice fish", he said, startling them. There wasn't much else to say, so he continued upstream.

The guide instructed the sport to hold off casting as they drifted past me. I don't think they'd seen David at all until after they'd caught the fish under his nose. For me, it underscored the role a guide can play in learning new water, local customs. I'll be the client in Labrador; I wonder what I don't know.

"It's okay to grin ear-to ear," I told them as they drifted by. "It was a nice fish."

"Anyone else ahead?" the guide asked me. I could see he felt awkward about the whole thing.

"Not with us. I don't know otherwise. Might be an angler on every corner." I laughed so he could tell I was just teasing him. "I doubt it," I added, "there was no one parked but us."

In that surreal, stretched time that is an angling evening, the drift boat took so long to pass that they noticed my cane and Hardy reel and commented, and we even had time to pass information on about getting a blue vest like mine for his girlfriend. The guide believed that my little rainbows were more likely young steelhead, a compelling thought. Of course there should be young steelhead here. The river suddenly became clearer. There was more depth around than just the measure of my feet below the water's surface.

I climbed out and followed the path to catch David. Mosquitoes came out about seven. The closest we came to the big brown was a suspicious wake in the same general area on our way back downstream. We could have fished later, but we were both content with our first exploration.

<u>July 14th, Monday</u>

A great morning to watch the few white clouds, unspoiled and headstrong, race across the blue sky. There's a brisk wind as the front moves on, promising a perfect day. Too bad we haven't mounted a wind turbine up on the top of the silo. Better yet, an observation deck. Just twenty feet across open air but even with the metal roof of the white block silo is a diamond shaped window at the peak of the barn's south-facing gambrel. That was my 'high hide' when I was growing up, my fort with a view of my world.

In the winter it was simple to scramble up the hay mow to reach the open window. When the barn was empty in the early summer, the climb was more like a jungle gym or like rock climbing. Wedging toes behind upright beams, I could move up the inside wall of the barn by pulling myself onto the horizontal beams. Attempting other maneuvers it was wise to omit in conservations with parents, I gained access to an incredible view sixty feet in the air perched on the highest hill on the farm. By hooking my inside leg around the diagonal ladder that led the last ten feet to the ceiling peak inside, I could safely lean outside over the window's sill supported on my elbows and watch the pigeons on the very top of the silo and the horses, cattle, and endless waves of hay stretching over rolling hills a half mile to the limit of the fields at the woods. There's a lot to be said for the big picture.

The errand list is growing shorter, the things to be done before we leave for Maine, then Labrador. We fixed a piece of sagging soffit after our breakfast on the porch. We need to fix a small door high on the back of the barn, one of those doors formerly for loading in hay. We'll nail it shut, probably, but not in this wind. David refined the lap on the ferrules on the Twins so they'd slide together a bit easier but not so much they'd be loose. We drove to town yesterday for dog food and treats for Effie and Midge, who ran through the fields earlier this morning, up and over the bales, but are now stretched out in the grass near the lilacs. Since we were already on the road, we continued on to Baldwin to drop off some bowling alley wax for the fly shop clerk who seems like a great guy and fishes the Wes Cooper cane rod. It feels good just to know he's there.

One way or another, we plan to stop by and see all of the assorted family and friends before we leave, just in case we don't make it back to Michigan after Labrador. Who knows? Maybe we'll just want to stay there.

July 22nd, Tuesday

We said good-by to Effie and Midge at 11 a.m.. It was hard. To them, we realized, it would just seem like any day that they napped together for the afternoon at home in Maine while we were off somewhere. It wouldn't even seem that weird at five, when their Aunt Barb whisked them off to her house, a mile away. Two weeks, for them, well, who knows? People say dogs have no sense of time. Since they came to live with us, we've tried to prepare them for our occasional absence. They're probably better prepared than we are. If we didn't have Barb, who loves them as her own, it would be nearly impossible to drive away.

By noon, we were in town at the fly shop. It might seem like we were getting a late day start on a long drive north, but we were actually leaving a half day early. With any luck, we'd have no troubles along the way, a gift of time in a place ripe for exploration. With trouble, like a flat or a road washout, we'd still not feel rushed to catch the float plane Friday morning. Actually, we really didn't expect any problems; we just couldn't wait any longer.

The stop thirty minutes later to see Mike and Linda was a given. We've never ventured far without checking in there last, a sure thing for a great send-off. Any apprehensions that might be lurking don't stand a chance against those two. Mike was all about the adventure. Linda was positive Effie and Midge would enjoy their vacation and that Barb would enjoy their sweet company.

Afterwards, on the Old Canada Road toward the Quebec border, we called Coh, who had

Kathy Scott

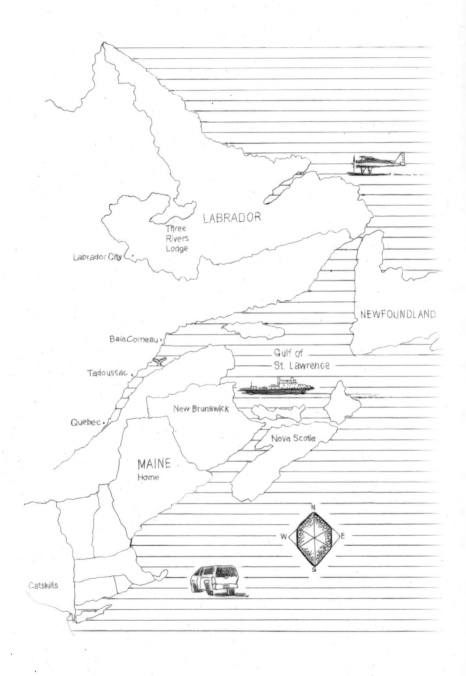

partnered on our travels since high school, virtually these past few years. Always call a good friend from the road.

David waited through his extended business greeting.

"Hey, Coh!"

"You assholes!" Coh laughed, dropping his business voice.

"Just checking in before we cross the border headed to Labrador," David explained casually.

There was a lot of laughing, and Coh said some other things. Distilled we knew he appreciated the ribbing as much as we would if he were heading out. Some friends are so close that they're along on the journey whether they're in the truck or not.

3:00 p.m.

Arrived at customs just beyond the outpost town of Jackman. Stopped at the Duty Free Store for five cigars, cheap Cubans for David to ward off blackflies. A Canadian customs officer looked at our passports; then she directed us inside. Another young officer left us in a waiting room while he disappeared into the office with the passports, but five minutes later he reappeared, gave the passports back, and we were back on the road. A sign explained that around 1810, one million French migrated to Maine's mills and farms through here. Interesting. Maine only has just over a million people today.

3:40 p.m.
Intermittent showers. Forest switched from the spruce bogs of the Maine border to new growth Quebec fir, spruce, and poplar. These woods hadn't been cut long ago.

3:43 p.m.
Lumber yard, makes sense. Green hay fields, fir, small French farms with long narrow fields stretching back from the road, followed by a cedar shingle mill.

4:30 p.m.
Leaving the town of Saint-Georges, a nice place with all the amenities. Street signs all in French.

5:00 p.m.
Sainte-Marie. Didn't stop; it was pouring rain. No interruption in the satellite radio so far. Just listening to local information: In 1642, Marie Grandmaison started a boarding house here, with the Ursulines, for locals and aboriginal peoples, who paid in eel, moose meat, and corn. She was known for her interest in fishing and in helping the local economy. 1642, well over 350 years ago.

5:30 p.m.

Quebec City, over four hundred years old, the only fortified city in North America. Easy to navigate, though, and breathtaking. There's a striking contrast between the castle-hotel that is the Chateau Frontenac overlooking the majestic St. Lawrence, the historic passageway to the Great Lakes, and the tiny quaint shops lining the back streets complete with flower boxes under the windows. Feels like going to Europe without leaving North America.

6:00 p.m.

The falls of the River Montmoracy are to the left, Isle d'Orleans to the right as we head east along the St. Lawrence on its northern shore. The tide is out. Grassy, out to choppy water.

6:30 p.m.

Sainte-Anne-de-Beaupre. The Shrine is the focal point here, a place of miracles some believe. For me, there's a family folk legend which says this is where my great-great grandfather Darius Scott found his young bride Sophie, native to this place, and swept her along on his journey from the British Isles to Ohio where my great grandfather and then my grandfather were born before driving a covered wagon far north into Michigan. Stopped at gas station. Weather still dark and moody; dug through daypack to switch out of my sunglasses to read French map.

<u>6:50 p.m.</u>

A high moose fence lines the road; well-trampled paths follow behind it. Altitude here is 740 meters, coastal mountains above the St. Lawrence with granite outcrops piercing endless fir. Too beautiful to go farther. Staying at a small campground, a family place with nice people, bilingual, enough trees to keep the small sites private, a few farm animals and a small river.

<u>July 23rd, Wednesday</u>

<u>6:45 a.m.</u>

On the road early. Exciting scenery. Stopped to photograph the rolling sea fog from the bluffs above Baie-Saint-Paul.

<u>7:15 a.m.</u>

Hydroponic tomatoes and a big square stern canoe for sale along the road near the artists' village of Saint-Joseph-de-la-Rive.

<u>7:20 a.m.</u>

11% grade down to another artists' community, Saint-Irenee. Riviere Jean-Noel tucked into town, small, clear, and rocky. Small steep roads up and out of town, winding between pretty little houses, bright shops, places to stay, and the characteristic church. A flagger at the edge of town near construction: Lentement / Arret (slow, stop).

7:30 a.m.
13% grade to La Malbaie for gas, a casino and resort town, very upscale. Sunny.

11:00 a.m.
Recovered enough to think straight. What's the single piece of equipment that would be impossible to replace on the road two days before a flight into a remote lodge in Labrador? My prescription sunglasses were on my face when the rain hit near Quebec City. Where are they now? I suspect everyone has a piece of gear that grows beyond usefulness, beyond giving confidence, to absurd importance. I don't remember ever fishing anywhere in the last five years without those glasses. It isn't easy finding the right fit, the right strength, the right combination of filtering bright light out yet allowing a heron's view deep into any water. Over time, they had become such a part of me that I'd worn them into movie theaters without noticing the difference. During allergy season, they masked my red eyes to the world. When I'm blue, they mask them, too. Suddenly, I found myself blind and exposed.

I searched the truck at the gas station: my day pack, the floor, behind the seat, every square inch, high and low, however unlikely. David finished filling the tank to find me in total meltdown. My heart was broken. All of the anxieties and excitement of months of waiting and preparation came sobbing out into four barely intelligible words.

"I lost my sunglasses."

He helped me search the truck again; then we tried the cell, which still worked. I called the campground. No one had turned in my sunglasses. David suggested that we could drive back ourselves and search the campsite. An hour later, when we still hadn't found them, our hosts were so gracious that they offered to call the gas station near St. Anne-du-Beaupre to ask them in French if they'd found the glasses. They hadn't.

By then, my reason was returning.

Back on the road, we tried a couple of stores without luck before I saw a Peche et Chasse sign. Fishing and Hunting. The elderly angler-hunter inside was so pleased that I did my best to speak French that he dug through the dusty recesses of that little shop until he found some goofy, wonderful, huge fishing glasses that slipped over mine. They covered most of my face, too, but they'd certainly work. He was very nice. Between his kindness and David's unflagging support, the new glasses, hideous and useful, became the first important lesson of the trip.

11:15 a.m.

Dramatic green mountains and perched small
lakes. Road clings to a cliff over the water. Black
Robe country, explored by Jesuits like Pere
Marquette. Cute baby black bear following a
glimpse of its mother into the brush. Enticing rock
climbing walls emerging from the dense,
dark spruce.

11:45 a.m.

Free ferry across the spectacular Riviere Saguenay
fiord, an arm of the St. Lawrence. Whales summer
here, always have. White belugas surfaced in the fiord,
close enough to be seen from the truck while waiting
in line for the ferry. Across the fiord is Tadoussac, a
1600 settlement of the French explorers.

12:45 p.m.

Picturesque falls and pedestrian suspension bridge
at Riviere du Sault au Mouton. St. Lawrence mud
flats nearby, littered with boulders.

2:15 p.m.

Betsiamites River, huge, on First Nation land;
Montagnais, the French called them, People of the
Mountains. Sand in the river, fish weirs downstream,
but no visible buildings. Fir and spruce.

2:45 p.m.

Huge earthen hydroelectric dam seven kilometers
before Baie Comeau.

3:30 p.m.

Baie Comeau has everything, food, gas, motels, and even a well-stocked, exclusive eyewear shop with polarized clip-ons exactly sized to fit my glasses. Having shed all pride hours earlier, I could only laugh at myself and consider the price the cost of my education. The town has two sections along the coastal highway. In the second, a signal light marks the corner for the road north.

3:50 p.m.

Winding our way north through forest on a shoulderless, black-topped road, curves lined with pink-gray granite. Climbing grades up to 12%; north really is up. Mountains all around. Clear, cold lakes are nestled in, small compared to the Hydro Quebec reservoir behind the Manic Two dam. Following the Riviere Manicouagan.

4:20 p.m.

Posted land on the left: Zec Varmin. What does that mean? Birch and fir give way to a lake. Emergency phone. The corridor to the North.

5:05 p.m.

Nice river east of the road between Manic Three and Lake Valiet, then some surprise boreal lakes with delicate tamarack among the rugged fir.

5:20 p.m.

50th Parallel! The big brook trout line. We're a bit giddy. Changes in latitude, changes in attitude.

6:00 p.m.

SOS phone again. Stopped to make a sandwich and test for blackflies; they're around, not bad. Five vehicles in the last two hours: one pick-up, two logging trucks, a motorcycle, and a convertible.

6:30 p.m.

Left Manic Five after filling the tank and checking out the store and motel. Clean, tidy, and nice, but very much the outpost, hydroelectric facility. The dam is huge beyond imagining, with a modern interpretive center. Series of switchbacks in the road

to climb to the level of the top, where there's an
elevated road over an equally unimaginable overflow
route for an untold volume of water. Good gravel
road, though. Truck hauling a manufactured home
escorted by guide cars lets us pass.

7:52 p.m.
Beautiful and sinuous road, sometimes pavement,
sometimes dirt. 51st Parallel.

8:30 p.m.
Lingering twilight. Pulled off the main road, down
to a found camping place among bottle-brush
spruce but mostly open.

July 24th, Thursday

4:30 a.m.
Fully light out, enough to write a mental note to
myself: sleeping in the front seat of this truck is not
especially comfortable. In our earliest camping days,
we called these places Canadian campgrounds, coined
for all of those free, gravel pit pull-offs in remote parts
of Ontario when we were college kids too poor to
pay for a place to stay, motel or campground. This
one was, as David predicted, clear of blackflies at
dark. We might be immersed in them soon enough.
No mosquitoes, either, a high, dry, open place. We
could just hear the rumble of a rare truck on the road

through the boreal wall between us. David moved
to the back of the truck about midnight, where we
usually sleep, but we were both too groggy to sort
out space for me back there, too, so I bet on finding
a comfortable position if I had the whole front. I lost
the bet, but I did sleep pretty soundly from, say, one
to four. Not sure I'd have slept much anywhere.

Other than losing my sunglasses, and then
losing David's hatlight while we were looking for
them, the trip has been wonderful so far. Robin
was right; this part of Labrador has the look and
feel of home, of Maine mountaintops and the
remote North Woods where we've spent much of
our lives. While we feel completely comfortable,
as if we belong here, there's no escaping the deep
excitement of knowing that this isn't home,
and these black spruce, and this caribou moss
blanketing the granite below them, stretch on into
the most remote places on the Continent.

Interior Labrador, the place of adventures
and adventurers. We've read their stories. This is
the land that tested the great hearts of Leonidas
Hubbard and Dillon Wallace on their ill-fated
canoe expedition. An early mistake sent them up
the wrong route and into winter, and disaster.
Labrador's rivers and lakes form waterways which
long defied mapping, yet granted passage to their
native inhabitants. There's something irresistible

about them, about the waters ahead, which makes it easy to understand why Dillon Wallace would return, and why guide George Elson would, too, joining Hubbard's widow Mina in a 1905 version of The Amazing Race.

Still, we aren't being lured blindly by the romance of the place. Besides talking with Robin, there's a bit of good research under our belts. We'd flown over when hiking an arctic island farther north, and we'd skirted the interior, exploring along the southern and eastern edges. We've just never ventured into the real heart of this country.

5:30 a.m.
On the road.

5:35 a.m.
Camp Energie at Ressourse, a cute little stop with gas and food available.

6:05 a.m.
Crossed over the Torrent River. Not a lot of water, but fishable.

6:25 a.m.
The Riviere Beaupin is even nicer and looks very fishable. Didn't stop, though.

6:30 a.m.
The Hart-Jaune, a magnificent river. Junction here to a Hydro Quebec facility.

6:50 a.m.

Ghost of the construction town of Gagnon, pavement with curbs and sidewalks and little else. Oddly encouraging that nature is reclaiming this place. A pickup truck with a First Nation couple stopped, so we did, pulling alongside to talk. No other traffic yet today. They wondered about the time and distance to Baie Comeau. I couldn't help but wonder where they'd come from, north.

7:00 a.m.

52nd Parallel. Official start of the taiga, the sometimes boggy, often rocky, always coniferous, harsh and breathtaking forest of the Northern latitudes.

7:30 a.m.

Burn area, both sides of the road.

7:40 a.m.

Second SOS phone of the morning. Quite Iron property, followed by River Peebles, nice. Cabin with a boat and anglers and two more pick-ups.

8:00 a.m.

Started crisscrossing the railroad tracks, moving on and off gravel and pavement. Two loons flew over.

8:30 a.m.

All corridors have converged: road, railroad track, powerlines. Traffic report : a black fox crossed the road.

8:45 a.m.

Stopped at wide gravel pull-off by a pond to raid the cooler and take in the view. Above the black spruce, in the distance, there's a mine shaft rising above the trees.

9:15 a.m.

Orange river, orange lake with orange logs, and a huge mine. Payloaders parked here look tiny. Ore train with engines at both ends. SOS phone.

9:44 a.m.

Labrador-Newfoundland border.

The Two Seasons Inn would be hard to miss. We followed the pavement into Labrador City, and there it was, right next to the McDonalds. We hadn't actually expected to find a Mac's in Labrador City. Through the course of exploring, we heard that its hours can be intermittent; when the mine needs people, many of the other businesses shut down. Mechanics are especially hard to find, according to a fellow traveler with a classic camping van on the blitz.

We checked in early at the Two Seasons, then checked out the town. Two towns, really, Lab City and Wabush, home of the solid ground airport. Along with little homes and company-style housing presumably related to the mine, there are places we'll explore more when we come out: a

beautiful museum and performing arts center, a
visitors' center, and gift shop. We passed through
a sports shop to see what flies were featured and
bought some weighted coneheads. With the
warm temperatures, high seventies, forecasts for
higher, the trout could be deep. At the large and
well-stocked grocery, we stumbled onto a Three
Rivers Lodge van, and, therefore, Darlene. She
immediately impressed us as both friendly and
capable, the perfect emissary for the Lodge. She'd
been keeping an eye open for us, she said, and
wondered if we needed anything or if we had any
remaining questions. We chatted until her van was
loaded with the Lodge's supplies. She'd be giving us
a call at the inn in the morning when it was time to
drive a few blocks to the float plane base.

"The others are mostly here," she informed
us, "except for the last two. Planes, connections."
Darlene was definitely on top of things.

Back at the Two Seasons a tall, outgoing guy
in a fishing shirt greeted us in the lobby. Douglas
Broadwater correctly guessed that we were the
other anglers headed in the next day and invited us
to join them all for dinner here at the inn.

"Come, meet the Dearborn party," he suggested
wholeheartedly. "Or at least join us afterwards for
a drink."

We had assumed that we'd get along well with anyone who would vacation in the interior of Labrador, fly fishers being who they are, but this was working out very well. Darlene, then the Dearborns. Given the forecast, we wanted to repack, so we opted to meet after dinner. The cold weather gear we jettisoned for weight considerations on the plane; it looked like a fleece jacket each covered by rain gear would be fine. Darlene had said there was even some limited laundry service, so packing extra in case of mud or a dunking didn't seem important either. Our remaining clothes and related items we packed together into a single bag, our fishing gear in another. We still had time to meet the six present members of the Dearborn party: Doug and John being family friends of Dave Dearborn, Phillip was Dave's youngest brother, and Chris and Fred were Dave's sons. Their college roommate, Hunter, had yet to arrive with his father, Woody. That gave us eight of our ten to toast an early and smooth departure and call it a night.

July 25th, Friday

Of all the time spent waiting, the last moments are the longest. We were wide awake at 4:30 in the premature light of the Labrador dawn. We packed the truck and walked to Mac's, then ate back in the room. We watched the weather forecast, cloudy with showers for the next week, good for fishing, but warm. There was nothing else left to do. We watched reruns of Andy Griffith, trying to remember the words to the title song. We'd hadn't even realized there were title words until we'd stumbled on them on a CD of fishing music, something like "Take down your fishin' pole and meet me at the fishing' hole." Darlene saved us by knocking on our door.

"We're all ready, but no rush. Take your time," she directed us cheerfully. "Drive over to the plane – yous went there yesterday, right? – and just put your luggage by the scales. I'm going to weigh the bodies first, not individually, but the whole group. Then the luggage."

We followed her to the lobby where she guided the Dearborns toward the van and led the way to the water. Our truck fell into line with the other vehicles parked to one side, some probably anglers, one Robin's. The last of my traveling twelve of diet soda tumbled out the passenger door to self-destruction, soda spraying everywhere. I took it as a sign I shouldn't take any. Just as well, it turned out. Our collective weight required some luggage remain for the Beaver which would bring in supplies, along with Hunter and Woody, later that day. We volunteered our clothes bag. Others made similar choices, and we were ready.

"Have yous ever taken off in an Otter before?"
Darlene asked us as the luggage was being loaded.
We hadn't. "It's so smooth, you won't know when it
happens," she promised. Smooth or rough, I didn't
care. Flying in a de Havilland Otter. How cool was
that? David had been looking the plane over with
an engineer's eye.

"De Havilland Otter," he pointed out the
characteristics to me. "If the Beaver is the half ton
truck of float planes, they say, the Otter is the one
ton truck."

The pilot met us at the end of the dock, plane side.

"I need to load you according to size," he said.
We all laughed as David, Fred, and I stepped
aside, and everyone made Doug board first. He
was directed into the co-pilot's seat, best seat in
the house. Then we filed in one after another, left
and right, everyone with a window seat, luggage
secured fore and aft. We taxied farther out onto
the lake, revved the engine up and down and up
and down, then brought it up to full roaring speed
again. We taxied again until David leaned across
from his seat, his mouth near my ear, to tell me
that we were in the air. I couldn't have guessed by
the ride or the height over the water. We slowly
climbed above the lake, above the black spruce, out
of sight of the Wabush mine and turned northeast.

At that moment, there was no place on Earth I'd rather be.

The roar of the Otter's engine prevented much conversation, but the important things were obvious. Fred, behind me, pointed out a black bear not that far below. David pointed to caribou trails worn through the moss on an esker. The ceiling held at 600 feet, cloudy as promised, but we flew gracefully below it. The land rose up nearer the plane as we shouldered the only real mountain between us and the Woods River system. The white, blue, and green flag of Labrador was inspired by all of this, a sprig of black spruce, the wealth of lakes and rivers, the simplicity of the wild landscape.

Endless dark spruce gave way to a sparser look, nudging the tree line. Caribou moss, really a lichen, carpeted openings in a light yellowish green, alders and willow shrubs a medium, brushy green. Granite from the roots of time emerged here and there, still fresh, and the patterns of muskeg and water decorated broad expanses. Lakes, lakes, everywhere, and beautiful rivers, some like mirrors, some roaring and exciting. Bogs with pools, then arching rock whalebacks. Braided caribou trails etched onto the landscape. I leaned on the daypack on my lap and rested my forehead against the window, my chin on my hand. For 150 miles, it was impossible to look away.

A small gathering of red-roofed buildings came into view below us. The Three Rivers Lodge: main lodge, cabins, boathouse, living quarters, generator shed. In a group of guides and camp staff awaiting our arrival on the dock below, I found Robin, and pointed him out to David and to Dave Dearborn, who, it turned out, had arranged this trip as a birthday present for his sons Chris and Fred. We taxied in to introductions and laughter all around. Frances and Dot, Darlene's aunts, made me feel especially welcome. So much fun, but out of place, to see Robin here and not at the Great Waters Expo, although this is where he seems most at home. Odd, too, to find Midwest Fly Fishing Magazine in our tidy Labrador cabin; it made me smile to think how things work out. Tom Helgeson's Expo, put on by his magazine, was officially where our trip began.

We dropped our gear in the pine-paneled front room of our cabin, then followed the wooden walkway to the main lodge where we joined Robin at the long table for a first good talk. Gradually, we were joined by everyone else. Ham and cheese sandwiches materialized as the camp manager Kevin briefed us about safety, the catch and release practice, and who'd be with which guide that day. I hadn't thought we'd go out so soon. David and I would be with Mark at the Lower Eagle Rapids, and Chris and Fred would be with Anthony at

Upper Eagle. The picture was emerging, life for
the next seven days: the Lodge would assure we'd
eat and sleep well, our new friends promised lively
camaraderie each evening, and the guides would
take care of our safety and location. All we had to
do, pretty much, was fish. We geared up. I'd fish
one Twin with the 8-weight line, David the other
with the 7-weight.

Mark motored us to the part of the Woods
River system that is Crossroads Lake, directly in
front of the lodge, and headed east. The new 40-
horse, Honda 4-stroke motor purred the Lund
Alaskan along quietly enough to talk over, but
I was pretty much speechless, taking it all in,
memorizing landmarks, trying to grasp the vast
scale of it all. At the Eagle, he idled us in over
boulders so we could climb out onto the bank.
We pulled the Twins from their cases and rod
sacks. I slipped mine together, sighted through the
guides to make sure it was straight, then secured
the reel and pulled out some line. A quick glance
found some soft moss amidst the Labrador tea,
a plant we know in Maine but is so wonderfully
native here. I set the butt of the rod there, doubled
over my line, and threaded it through the guides.
There might have been three blackflies, nothing
my quick application of DEET couldn't handle.
Made me a little sorry that I folded under a bit
of apprehension, a fear that I'd wimp out in the

face of hordes of them – it's happened in Maine in June before, me retreating inside, private defeat. The best defense against the unknown up here had seemed to be a solid offense, so I was hopped up on my first day adrenaline and Benadryl.

By then, Mark had set David up in a likely spot and returned to guide me slightly upriver. My legs were feeling pretty shaky, but I hoped I wouldn't have to admit it. Mark pointed to a near boulder, just a hop over rushing water.

"I'll never make it," I blurted out. Admit it now, or die, I thought. I caved easily in the face of the biggest rapids I'd ever fished.

"Think you can trust me?" Mark asked. "I can get you there."

"Are you kidding me?" I laughed. "My life is totally in your hands. I'm here to fish, and I'll go anywhere you can take me. Seriously. Your call." In truth, it was a head-heart total agreement. My head said that this guy would keep me safe, or he wouldn't be guiding. My heart said that if I was going to take some risks, there was no better place to do it. No ego to bruise on my part; I couldn't get out there any other way.

Mark stepped into the roar, offered a hand, and I leapt for the boulder. Piece of cake.

Mark tied on a fly. This was much harder for me to accept, but I did. If I lost my first fish on a fly I'd tied on poorly, I probably would have been disappointed. Actually, I'd have been very disappointed.

Then, the first cast. I tossed the fly to a lie behind the next boulder, a likely spot. Nothing. That was the first time it crossed my mind that I could actually be skunked in Labrador. Brook trout are no more an entitlement here than they are anywhere. Two hours, much boulder hopping and wading on Mark's arm against the current, and three flies later, we stopped for a snack in the boat, then crossed to the other side. Mark was showing me the slow end of a steady run, a great spot, I hoped, when we noticed David's rod finally bent. He thought he'd hooked the bottom, but we ran down to net (Mark) and photograph (me) a 3-pound brook trout.

David beamed as he passed along his advice, "They're deep."

Mark switched my fly to one of his own, a weighted sculpin, barbless. All of the flies we used were either pinched or barbless to begin with, a rule of the lodge we found particularly appealing. Learning Labrador, learning new rods, learning big trout barbless, why not all at once? I tossed the sculpin into the run. As soon as it sank, something heavy bent my rod. I reacted to the incredible pressure, and then it was gone. At least I'd felt it.

By then, we were all hot in the intense and unexpected late day sun, and time ran out. We motored back to camp for hot showers in our cabins before joining the others for a complete roast beef dinner and shared stories. Fred and Chris, on the rapids above us, had done well. How? We had trouble teasing the details out of them at first, but it sounded like each released four or five nice trout, say, three, four pounds.

"Usually I'm about the journey," Chris quipped, "but, to hell with that, I want fish!"

Laughter all around the long table. Their college friend Hunter has arrived, though his luggage has not. He's making due while it catches up. Since his father, Woody, is a northern pike fisher, talk drifted to the potential for evening fishing near the Lodge. Apparently, the guides are all willing to go back out after supper, and the lake trout and pike fish well, the trout often on dries. Kevin concluded the meal with the guide assignments for the next day, tailored to each guest's taste and approval. David and I were to be flown to Second Rapids, sharing a ride with part of the Dearborn party since four of them and two guides would be overnighting downstream at Fifth Rapids. Our guide would be Anthony, Fred and Chris's guide from today.

July 26th, Saturday

*T*he generator purred to life at 6 a.m., but I was already awake. Amazing to be so comfortable. No need for the white nets furled and waiting over the beds or the wood stove. We had matching sheets and pillow cases, a fleece blanket, and a comforter, just right to snuggle into during last night's wind and brief but welcome cool rain. The cabin was already light and airy from the skylights and the bright knotty pine.

We joined Robin and Fred on the porch of the main lodge to relax over coffee and watch the day begin over the lake. Still no bugs to worry about. Frances asked Robin to ring the breakfast bell, and we assembled around plates of sausages, fresh fruit, and several cereal choices.

An hour later, we were in waders and vests, PFD's in hand for now, the Twins in their cases. We met the elder Dearborn (Dave) with Fred on the dock. While we waited for the float plane to land, we talked fly fishing, the first common denominator. Dave had fished the Gunnison River in Colorado with Fred, who lives in that state. They'd had a memorable trip, though Dave thought it was fairly big water. He'd used a wading staff, one much like ours. David mentioned that at our fly shop, Mike had recommended using dubbing wax to keep the joints from binding. Dave's had stuck already, and we offered some wax when they returned from Fifth. Our friends Mike Canazon and Jeff Hatton regularly fish the Gunnison and had invited us along after the Colorado rodmakers' gatherings, so I was curious about the river. Fred thought that if we could handle the Labrador rapids, the Gunnison would be no problem. I had a better idea why he and Chris did so well at Upper Eagle. Practice.

The De Havilland Beaver flew over, circled around to grace the water, and taxied in. I climbed into the sling, the bush seat in the rear of the plane, David next to the window in front of me, Fred next to him in the middle of the seat, and Anthony at the door. Dave Dearborn joined the pilot up front. What a way to start the day- in a float plane with a bird's eye view of Interior Labrador! It

takes a couple of days to begin to understand that
the Woods River system is flowing. Eagle River,
Rick's Run, and Victoria combine upstream of the
lodge on Crossroads Lake, one of a series of huge
lakes which are swells in the Woods. A short hop
overland reconnects with the system as it turns
south, the series of rapids serving as roaring rocky
reminders that all the waters move downstream.
We spotted Second Rapids on our way downriver,
landed at Fifth Rapids where Chris, Phillip, and two
guides awaited Dave and Fred for their overnight,
and then waved to them all as we flew off again.
David moved up front with the pilot, and I took his
window seat on the bench with Anthony.

Second Rapids is so open and wide that there
were still no bugs, and I was becoming my normal
self enough to be happy that I wouldn't be risking
the finish on my rod dissolving from DEET on
my hands. I hadn't even thought of that with
everything going on yesterday. I approached the
water more rationally, too. The puzzle was to
discover how to catch a big brook trout, simple as
that. The pieces were few: recognize where what I
already know fits in, scan the water and conditions
for likely places to drop my fly, pick the right fly,
listen to the guide.

The Beaver had dropped us off at a green,
North Woods canoe, so Anthony motored us

across the lake to the left side of the foot of Second Rapids. These rapids were even wilder from the water than the air, and I'd thought them impressive then. Trust the guide. He thought I should start from the boat, casting to the run just under the willows near shore. He flipped his long net upside down, set the butt of the handle firmly on the bottom, grasped the curve of the wood at the top of the net with both hands, and stepped out of the boat. Completely stable, he led David into the foot of the rapids. I swallowed and looked away. Fish the willows, that's your goal.

The fish hadn't heard about my personal goals, though, so Anthony waded back and pulled me in the canoe up the side of the rapids. He stood me on a rock not so hard to reach after all.

"Any advice?" I asked him. "I've never fished here before."

He looked in my fly box, pronounced them all pretty good, and pointed out the run in front of me. What more could he do? Here, as everywhere, fish bite when you figure out the right fly, and you try all likely patterns until you do. I decided to urge him to go back down to David, mid-river at the foot of the whitewater, which would let me experiment a bit. My 8014 Guide and I would work this out.

From my good solid rock, a flat granite boulder on the brink of very deep and very fast water, I started to piece things together. The depth of the water a foot away made for a smooth run about twenty feet long and ten feet wide. Above and below it, jutting boulders turned the water into white standing waves. What lay in the depths below them, a deep secret. Anything that moved into the run, fish or fly, would be in plain view. Reasoning that the fish wouldn't want to be seen and that the weather was uncommonly warm, I guessed that the clear water would only hold fish very deep, and, even so, I should be able to see them. I couldn't. That meant the fish, if there were fish, and Anthony said there were, must be under the shield of the turbulence.

That same rough water would mask a sloppy cast. For a choice of flies, I decided to start with a dry, something I do fairly well, and drop a Royal Wulff in the last moment of whitewater upstream, let it drift across the glassy water, and retrieve it as it disappeared below in the froth. I double checked my knot, finally hooking the fly on a ring on my vest and giving it a tug. The 2X tippet held tight. I lofted my line into the air, judged the distance, and sent it into the backcast, only to snarl the leader in a willow behind me. Even without Anthony, I could make it back to shore balanced with my wading staff to unhook it. I tested the knot again once I reclaimed my big rock and carefully false cast twice, then set the dry down roughly where I'd hoped. I didn't breathe as it floated quickly past me. At least I had a better idea of the real time it took to travel past, I thought, and cast it again. I knew nothing was rising and that the brook trout seemed deep, so I wasn't worried. Plan B was to fish an olive conehead woolly bugger, Anthony's idea. I managed not to hook it behind me but did have to duck once as it sped by. Finally, I mastered the micro-climate of wind and water that is fishing in rapids and plunked it into the head of the run, then stripped it back from the base. On the third try, I noticed something following it as it reappeared under the glass. The brook trout was just so big, I hadn't really recognized it before.

Anthony had moved out to retrieve David about the time I decided the fly had turned cold and switched to the same pattern in black. I also decided to get a bit bolder with my casting, tested the close water again just in case, then put all of my arm into both the back and forward casts, hurling the 8-weight line with the bugger across the pool into the whitewater, letting the fly sink and race down with the current toward the rocks below, and stripping it back fast.

Twice a magnificent trout followed it back to my feet, where I ran out of room to strip. I was excited.

David and Anthony arrived, and Anthony was very patient with my story.

"Did you see it? Was it really a trout?" he asked. David had hooked two northern pike accidentally when he was wading upstream. They were around.

Fortunately, both David and Anthony were still close enough to witness the bend in my rod and the beautiful, probably 3-pound, trout I pulled into view. No one ever explains how to land these things, and I was suddenly at a loss. Should I let this one run back into the fast water, the strong current? That didn't seem wise. But it was deep and almost directly below me and not giving way.

"Feel free to tell me what to do," I called out.

Anthony was at my elbow, net ready, when a brook trout that made mine look like a minnow showed up, and we watched through the glass window of the pool as it bullied its way over, grabbed the protruding end of my black woolly bugger, and jerked the barbless fly out of my trout's mouth.

"Did you see that? Did you see that?" This was from Anthony, not me, though he took the words out of my mouth. "I'd heard about this before, but that was something!"

Inarguable.

At lunch, a mini-cooler for each of us packed by Dot and Frances, I asked about all of the things

I should have done. I'd never played a fish on the reel and could have let the trout run out the slack, maybe, then let the drag and reel help me out, except that the fish was already at my feet, just deep and stubborn. We all agreed that there wasn't much anyone could do if the trout were tag-teaming against the anglers. It put us in a great mood, the wonder of it all. Even losing a fish in Paradise is fun, and I'd had witnesses to a story that would never have held up otherwise. Anthony told us other tales and shook his head in mock disapproval over Fred and Chris on the Upper Eagle the day before. It was obvious he enjoyed being with them.

"Those fellas, they were jumping from rock to rock, going everywhere. They caught some nice fish," he told us, expanding on the stories we'd all heard together over dinner. The guides sit together at the table next to the ten of us, all a family, and they were drawing us in. As my ears grew more accustomed to his musical, Newfoundland accent, I thought I heard something about one of them falling in, and maybe a broken tip. I think these stories were to persuade me that I wasn't entirely wrong having some respect for the power of the rapids but that I would gain some confidence and technique with experience. Anthony dug through the little cooler and handed David something to pass to me.

"Give this to she," he said.

It was my own banana bread, baked with no nuts.
A little gesture, but the warmth was undeniable.
Frances and Dot had been concerned about my
nut allergy and were eager to make me comfortable
despite it at the big shared meals. To take the extra
effort to send along a treat especially for me was
particularly touching, out on a canoe seat with David
and Anthony, Second Rapids inches away.

After lunch, we fished up that side of the rapids
and crossed while fishing the top from the canoe.
It wasn't easy; Anthony was in the water most
of the time. His boulder hopping in current was
as admirable as his ability to maneuver us into
position. We fished down the other side and crossed
back at the foot. Then I waded back out to my Big
Rock. Who'd have thought I'd get another chance?

I tied on something similar but different, just in
case trout have memories. I didn't want that three
pound brook trout which took the woolly bugger,
anyway. I wanted that gigantic friend of his. A black,
conehead nymph about an inch long and weighing
a ton seemed right. I checked again to remember
where the willows were, put all of my arm into it,
and cast as far across and upstream as I could. The
fly kerplunked into the whitewater and disappeared
immediately. The line swung downstream, and
I started to strip it back toward the glassy pool.
Something big took it hard and ran down the rapids.

"Fish on! Fish on!" I called out. There was so
little line stripped in that the fish had put himself
onto the reel, and David and Anthony coached
me as I played him. At one point, I worried over
a mad dash he made out directly away from me,
too near tangling over boulders or cutting the line,
and asked Anthony to land it, just so I could see

it. He refused, a great call. He instructed me to just let it run, take my time. I finally guided it back where Anthony scooped it up with the long arm of his net and held it securely so David could snap a few photographs. It was just over twenty inches and a football. Anthony calculated its weight at 5-pounds; girth squared times length over 800 equals the weight. I watched it afterwards resting near the bottom of the glassy pool as I rested at the top.

We ended the evening, after supper, with a nice talk with Robin, Doug, John, and Hunter about the day, about fish, cane, furled leaders, and good music. David borrowed some scouring powder from Frances to rub clean the male ends of our ferrules, assuring a good fit the next day. Woody retired early, but we weren't far behind. Hunter's clothes still haven't arrived in Labrador City, though he doesn't really seem to care.

July 28th, Monday

Yesterday's trip to Rick's Run started with motoring across the lake in an open Lund with Quintin, stashing the boat, and carrying our gear a half mile on a small path winding through silent black spruce and tamarack. Our steps were softened by blankets of caribou moss; caribou trails crossed ours. Labrador tea stood knee high. Occasional patches of cloudberry or bakeapples, begged us to stop and sample the orange fruit. Kevin had told us that the French found them here and asked something like ba qu'appelle?, what is this called? The delicious cloudberries became bakeapples.

We loaded a canoe at the end of our portage then picked our way upstream between boulders to admire the beauty of the rapids of Rick's Run, named after Robin's brother, now gone. It was a day when the scenery outdid the fishing; the peace of the portages dwarfed the music of the water. It had been interesting to be on foot, to smell the warmth of the land, to find traces of the animals there. We both caught brook trout, but, on our way back, Quintin mentioned that the expanse between the rapids held Northern pike. Trolling for pike on cane. Natives, they share these waters with the trout, but prefer the quiet runs, the eddies, the lakes. As strong swimmers, the brook trout easily negotiate life in the protective rapids. At home in Maine, pike aren't native and spell disaster when slipped into trout waters with no Labrador scale rapids to protect them. Quintin fixed me up with a bite guard and something long that was made of white bunny. I flipped my cane rod over every few minutes, reel up, reel down, to prevent it from taking a set. My pike had a bite scar on its back from a much larger cousin.

Knowing we'd be flying out for two days this morning made last night's stories at the lodge all the more interesting. So easy to like these people. The Dearborns were alive with tales of Fifth Rapids, the beautiful new cabin on the point of a high ridge, nearly a 360-degree view. Their family closeness is always visible. Chris, a dad himself, called home from the satellite phone after dinner to hear their voices. Then he, Fred, and Hunter went out trolling with a guide, maybe hitting the late evening white fly hatch.

"Trolling for lake trout and drinking beer, the way fishing is supposed to be," announced Hunter as they left. Good humor for anglers who aren't used to boulder hopping and casting all day, days in a row. My arm was holding up, but I could see the writing on the wall.

This morning, we swapped our first bush pilot for a new one, also named Fred. He arrived with Hunter's clothes bag and some good stories to tell. A lean, dashing character in a brown leather jacket and blue jeans, he flies a 1956 Beaver which, he told us confidently, is built like a tank and will last another fifty years. A native of French Quebec, he's also an engine mechanic, a great winter job for a pilot, we thought. He used to fly whale watching trips but prefers the interior to the sightseeing flights.

"Pratt and Whitney radial engine," David pointed out to me as we climbed in. When we had lived on the northern Maine border with New Brunswick, it seemed like half of the small town's population had either moved to Connecticut to work for Pratt and Whitney or knew someone who had.

"People wonder why it smokes when it's first started in the morning," Fred said with affection. "It's because it's a radial. The engine oil drains down overnight in the bottom cylinder where the spark plug is on the bottom."

As he carefully noted the time in his flight book, a record of the engine hours, he told us about a friend of his who had been flying to Schefferville a few years earlier, a mining outpost north yet of Labrador City, and had been delayed by weather for a while. Then he flew out, choosing the more narrow of two passes in the barrier mountain. At the last minute, he'd decided to turn back, clipped a wing, and died. Some unfortunate decisions.

"This is safe if you keep records so you can maintain the plane and if you are careful," he explained. "I used to ride a motorcycle, but that I gave up. Too dangerous."

We laughed and liked him immensely. We flew past Second Rapids again; I could see my Big Rock. Two eagles flew below us. Fred's landing

technique involved getting the floats on the deep
water as quickly and safely as possible; better to hit
a shallow water rock in a taxi then while coming
in. When we'd reached the sandy shore just below
the outpost cabin at Fifth Rapids, Mark, again our
guide, climbed out on the pontoon, then entered
the water to turn the plane around. We off-loaded
our gear and watched as Fred taxied out and flew
away, leaving us there.

The cabin was new; Robin had built it himself,
and he'd only owned the lodge eleven years, leasing
more area than his guests could ever explore. This
isn't the only outpost, but it is the only cabin,
home away from home. It's perched on a bluff, a
high peninsula, accented by tamarack and black
spruce, Labrador tea for shrubbery, and tall pink
fireweed and low white bunchberry blossoms for
flower beds. A relatively open ridge runs behind
it, past the small shed housing the generator. A
trail continues on, used by wolves (judging from
some scat) and a black bear, which had ripped the
door off the generator shed the week before and
made off with the gas can. Mark had found it still
dripping gas from the teeth holes. Understandable,
we thought. Effie and Midge like to chew plastic
soda bottles.

The cabin has a boardwalk along one side
leading to the porch. A thick rope serves as the

railing. The view for anglers pulling on waders or watching stars come out is of the Labrador flag come alive, the blue water, the greens of small, hardy conifers, even the sprig of black spruce. Inside, the cabin is characteristically bright, pine with big windows by the table in the front room, which also serves as the kitchen. A handsome caribou head mount oversees the refrigerator. To the left, a string of three smaller rooms all have welcoming twin beds, the first two rooms for guests, the third for guides. Back between the guides' room and the bathroom is the satellite phone.

We stowed our gear and followed Mark to a green Scott canoe with a small, 15-horsepower motor leashed to the alders. The plan was to fish Third and Fourth Rapids and save Fifth for Tuesday before we flew back to the lodge. Fifth is so close to the cabin, we could reach it even in bad weather. In fact, we had to pass through it heading up river. Mark motored as far through the boulders as he could, then jumped out to pull us ahead through standing waves and jutting rock. Finally, at the top, the canoe bumped so many boulders that David and I climbed out, too, and waded as best we could against the current with uncertain footing, holding on to the canoe. The water would be a few inches deep, then suddenly two or three feet would drop away. It was so much fun trying to boulder hop upstream with an arm hooked over the gunwale behind Mark (who later told us about being a weightlifter, good thing). I laughed so hard when my feet were swept away that I could only hang by my elbow while David, behind me, called ahead to Mark, over the roar of the rapids, that we'd better stop. The second time, I gave up and crawled back into the canoe. Along that stretch somewhere, I lost my fear of the rapids.

The run up to Fourth goes through a expansive part of the river, a seeming lake, where we found two loons with two chicks on their backs. Fourth Rapids is a wide open stretch of mostly quickwater. Mark pulled us through easily, and we motored on to Third. There we anchored to wade up the shallow side of a willow island. I recognized it as a familiar scale with familiar lies and offered to stay and enjoy it while Mark continued upstream with David. I pulled my wading staff out of its holster and felt right at home. They made their way to the head of the island and found a Labrador-sized brook trout waiting under the willows on the deep water side. I was releasing little fish, so I missed the take when David caught a 5-pound brook trout, the perfect mate to mine on Second Rapids.

We had to pass on Fourth Rapids on the return run. The wind had come up across its open water, and Fifth seemed like a better call. The air and the water continued to warm; David measured the

water at 69 degrees at one point, one degree shy of
Robin switching us all to lake trout and pike. The
die-hard conservationist in both of us made us
less eager to stress the trout as the afternoon wore
on. This evening's walk exploring the esker ridge
where the cabin is perched was just as interesting.
There is endless appeal in the subtle secrets of the
North, the single raven rok through the silence, the
creeping snowberry, a tuft of fur from a snowshoe
hare. Stories in whispers. We walked back along
the caribou trials breathing in the heart of this
place. We love the solitude, the seclusion. A total
of sixteen other people in our world of three rivers,
and none closer than the lodge, a very long canoe
ride or a plane flight away. The first sprinkles from
the approaching cold front started just as we called
it a night.

July 31st, Thursday

T-bone steak night, followed by the last evening
with our Three Rivers friends. A week either flies by
very fast or becomes a lifetime, or, in this case, both.
We were joined by Robin's son Matt and a friend
who had flown in on the supply flight to help with
the log addition to the main lodge. Robin already
had the walls up. Over the meal Cliff, a guide
who'd found us fish willing to take dries at Vezina

Narrows and who indulged us a small stream break on little PJ's River, announced the score of the Yankee-Red Sox match up to the expected rowdy comments from the New England guests. Then, the Dearborns concluded the day with their customary game of Liar's Dice, a longtime family game they persuaded Doug and John to join. I'd sat in a couple of nights ago, learning more about the people around the table than the game.

In Liar's Dice, the first person rolls the dice but keeps them hidden under a cup. He makes a strategic call about them, potentially not true, like "two 2's and a 3". The next person either doesn't believe him and says "I doubt it" and lifts the cup or accepts his word and the dice to manufacture his own story, say "two 2's and a 4". If a disbeliever is wrong, he loses a sugar packet (a high stakes game). If the disbeliever is correct, the one with the dice loses a packet. If the dice are higher, it's okay (two 2's and a 5). The game is less important to them, though, than the years and places they've played it together, holidays, summers at the lake.

I was patiently guided into the Dearborn clan but proved no match for a history of playing together growing up and now as time allowed. They subtitled the important plays and inside jokes for me with the stories behind them. In the course of the play, I learned that Dave, the patriarch, still lives in Massachusetts not far from Harvard, where he worked. Fred went to school with Hunter, but he's a counselor now in Colorado; pony-tailed Chris teaches constitutional law on the East Coast; Hunter splits his work between Florida and Virginia, though his father, Woody, lives in Ohio. Woody detailed the efforts to establish Lake Erie steelhead for David and me, a hugely successful story, he says. Doug, a persistently positive romantic, mentioned that he has a place in the Catskills when I described the class we teach for the museum there. John, it turns out, is on the Catskill Fly Fishing Museum's board of directors. Small, interesting world. Phillip, Dave's brother, also lives in Florida. He'd once been involved in producing a movie.

Divergent lives, converging here, enriching mine. The same goes for the guides. We spent days of one-on-one time in their good company. The common ground they share with their guests isn't just this place; they share a spirit willing to embrace it, to live life.

During a break in tonight's game, Chris stepped aside with Anthony, who'd carved some small figurines for Chris's children. Anthony can transform a small block of wood sometimes into a perfect little moose, maybe into a tiny axe embedded in a chopping block. His own children are nearly grown, and he shares with the

Dearborns a strong sense of family. One night, he patiently endured the intermittent connection of the satellite phone, talking two minutes, waiting thirty when the signal was lost, then trying again, until he heard their whole story of the new puppy back home on the island. The second time Anthony guided me fishing a nymph, the fly was tiny, maybe an 18, and the brook trout was about four pounds.

Cliff lives across the bay from Anthony in far northern Newfoundland, thirty minutes by boat, two hours by car. They guide together there, too. It's a place of moose, caribou, and Atlantic salmon, of hand-lining for cod. A dry fly guy with an outgoing personality, Cliff sees a raw day some people would call miserable as a rare opportunity to fish blue-winged olives. While we were out with him, David caught a 5-pound trout on either a 16 or 18, I didn't see the fly. I did see the big triangular mouth rising out of the water in slow motion. Cliff is loosely related to young Jordan, who lives next door at home, and who taught me how to direct the travel of a large trout on the end of my line by maneuvering the tip of my rod.

Quintin seems to be the youngest. We spent the least amount of time with him but enjoyed watching him interact at the lodge. Although he's quite quiet, he's also prone to fun. If he sees another guide is about to come through the door, he's likely to lock it, laugh, and run. Moose hunting is his speciality.

We fished today with Ned, a guide who is married to Dot, therefore brother-in-law to Frances, and Darlene's uncle. We joined him at the dock. Then, instead of motoring down the Woods, we traveled up past Rick's Run to the Eagle, where we'd started the week on the lower rapids. Arctic terns hovered and dived. We put ashore on the opposite side as before and hiked upriver through the sparse and spongy subarctic forest. Waxwings and bear scat revealed a blueberry patch, low and brushy, but the berries were mostly gone.

My arm was predictably sore – who fishes seven days straight? - but I cast into the Upper Rapids as best I could all morning, pausing in the afternoon to sit on a boulder and chat with Ned. We talked about Labrador; then I asked him about himself. His home is in Newfoundland, too, and he loves all things outdoors. Sixty-two, he's been on the water all his life. His father cooked on a cod ship; his parents are both in their eighties and still very much alive. He and Dot have five children (one girl) and six grandchildren. If he loved this place and those people before, he does so much more now. He feels he's been given a second chance at life since surviving a float plane crash.

It's troubling, he told me, how fast it happened, but he'd resolved that it was just one of those rare things, far less likely than a car crash, and he'd been flying ever since. I told him that I'd been a lot more concerned about not catching a fish or looking inexperienced in front of a guide than worried about the float planes.

"It may be old fashioned or superstitious, but no one catches much cod when the wind is in the northeast, either. You're doing good," he reassured me, "but your husband's doing better!" While we'd been talking, David landed another fish in front of us.

Ned seems born to be helpful. He's always at the dock to unload the float plane or greet guests; he made certain the emergency beacon was tripped after the plane crash. He showed me a great spot, a big boulder with a clear view to the bottom maybe eight feet below with plenty of room to cast. I found my footing, and looked down to see a tremendous fish, easily as big as the Second Rapids trout. What a great last fish it would make. Willing, too, at least at first. I pulled that barbless conehead nymph in front of him, and he grabbed the thing. As soon as I felt his weight on my Twin, I looked down to see his kype-jawed face suddenly pause and look up. I swear he was wise enough to know: angler, not supper. Despite my tension on the line, he shook his head fiercely, throwing the barbless fly out while I watched powerless to stop him.

"Okay," I conceded happily, "you win." I was fished-out anyway.

While I watched him resting, the fly dangled above the water behind me, and my usual size brook trout leapt out of the water and grabbed it. Too funny. I knelt to release him, a handsome ten-inch brook trout.

"Were you jealous, baby?" I asked him. No need to be. Little jewels were my first love.

As the Dearborns continued their lively game, David and I talked with Kevin and Frances. Kev asked us to fly out with Fred (the pilot) in the little Beaver, early, with Woody and Hunter, who had an early flight out of Wabush. Sounded like fun. The Otter would fly in to the lodge a little later, carrying the anglers in for the next week's fishing, then bring the Dearborns out. We were curious about Kevin and Frances sledding in over the snow, about 150 miles up the river system, something they had done every year from their home in Lab City. That trip, they said, took three days by snow machine, stopping at remote cabins along the way. One winter, they were the last of a line of snowmobiles crossing snow-covered ice on one of the huge lakes when mechanical problems

separated them as darkness fell and the cold
deepened. Frances explained how Kevin had dug
them a snow cave out there on the ice, and they
stayed warm with a little emergency stove as the
wind howled overhead. Instead of turning their
backs on the North, they were just reassured they
could handle it.

That pretty much sums up this trip for me.
Take what I already know from the woods of
Maine, brook trout and a little about fly fishing,
and apply it to a new, wilder place. The casting
technique, line management, careful knots, and
well-inspected tippet are all attainable, especially
with practice. Finding the fish and choosing the
fly only get better with experience. The same for
wading in rapids, although it sometimes feels like
art. A powerful brook trout cutting the line on a
rock, a second trout snatching the fly out of the
first trout's mouth, or a fish so wild that it defies
catching: those things are just a matter of luck,
and, to me, fall into the Good Stuff category, an
honor to witness. Fishing the Twins here was
such an added bonus, split cane fly rods we'd made
together, a different taper, bigger that we'd made
before. They'd been an ideal choice after all, so
integrated into our Labrador days they'd almost
disappeared from notice.

David and I were talking about the Twin rods as we wandered out onto the porch where Robin was enjoying the nightfall. We joined him one last time, sitting in the glow of the evening, looking out across the water of Crossroads Lake. Stories went back and forth. He told us that Canadian biologists are trying to determine how far fish travel here, how long they stay resident. The guides will be tagging fish to help. We mentioned that Maine biologists are cataloging wild, purely native brook trout ponds. Studies, information, informed decisions. The Atlantic Salmon Federation and Trout Unlimited are helping remove dams on our Penobscot River in Maine. Here, prospectors are searching every corner; with a major discovery comes a push to dam, harnessing energy for refining, one maybe in the future of a river a bit north holding landlocked Arctic char. Oquossoc? We hadn't realized there were bluebacks nearby, but we were glad to hear it and hoped they fared better than ours. Back and forth, separate news but a connected part of the Big Picture; we shared our interest in all of it.

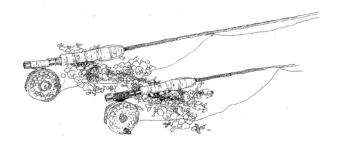

As the evening drew to a close, we realized we wouldn't actually need both of the Twins much longer. After this, if we found ourselves fishing in seven or eight-weight rivers, we'd probably make another taper, try a different rod. We knew what these could do, and would keep one. The other we offered to leave there with Robin, but he had another idea. Why not use it as a fundraiser, and buoy up one of those efforts we all supported? We agreed, but only if he'd let us add his name to the gift.

Kathy Scott

August 26th, Tuesday

*E*ffie and Midge went all rubbery and cuddly when we picked them up but were settled back in before we'd even finished thanking David's sister. We were overjoyed to be with them again, but, with more travel time confinement coming right up, we encouraged them to run some of the energy out of their systems. The moment we attached the bells to their collars, the pups were down the hill and off at full romp. Later, Midgey came back up the hill to find us, barking the news of her missing sister. We couldn't find Effie for a while, either. The three of us, David, Midge, and I, combed the nearby woods and listened for the bell. We were almost back to the house when we discovered our dedicated Effie sitting absolutely still on point beneath a tree about twenty feet from the kitchen window. Red squirrel.

As soon as we recovered from the two-day drive back to Maine, the last half dodging trees downed by fierce wind and rain, cafe au lait streams flooding the New Brunswick roads, we packed the two up for a run back to Michigan. Midge must have missed us; she didn't even protest. All good things move on to the next good things, though, and we returned to Maine last week to get ready for fall, for school, for whatever else lay ahead.

Kathy Scott

The Jacks-in-the-Pulpit are wearing their bright red berries, another sign that we're going toward fall. David's mom always says that when the wind runs over the goldenrod, we're going toward fall. There's no wind here today, but the other signs will do: the flocking of wood ducks, young crows, and Canada geese; the last of the hazelnuts ripe, picky, and overlooked on the bushes at the edge of the clearing; a few spring peepers starting in again, confused by the length of day too similar to spring. A moose had crossed the trail to the beaver dam sometime before we walked Effie and Midge in this evening's cooler air. They're growing restless.

David called our Atlantic salmon biologist, Paul Christman, for a post-summer update. He recapped how high water had made checking the artificial redds nearly impossible after we had left in June but that they'd electro-fished as summer went on and found salmon fry everywhere. In some cases, they had discovered salmon babies where there had been no redds, at least none he'd had a direct hand in creating. As near as he could tell, some of the adult females that had been trucked upriver from the Lockwood Lift after they returned to the Kennebec must have created redds that stimulated male parr to become precocious. To have salmon returning to the river at all was amazing and gave us hope, but the run still wasn't a fraction of the historic number. We'd wondered what would happen with so few salmon trucked. How would so few males find so few females in so many miles of river? Precocious parr. Nature finds a way.

Brook trout have received some notice this summer, too. The stream survey has been in progress, and scores of old documents have been reviewed to discover which ponds and lakes have never been stocked. Heritage brook trout. More information in hand, decisions will have to follow this winter which will safeguard their fate.

Firewood was delivered today for the end of this winter, or, preferably, next fall. Three cords are already dried and tucked away for this year.

Tomorrow the kids come back to school. I dug out my black daypack, the one that I'd carried all over on the Labrador trip, intending to clean out and repack it for the morning. In the bottom of the black pack I found a small, black case, perfectly camouflaged, and in that case, my sunglasses. Astonished, I held them up for David to see.

"You didn't need them," he said.

Kathy Scott

September 10th, Wednesday

*T*he gathering of rodmakers in the Catskills takes place the weekend after Labor Day. As much as the students returning to school signals the beginning of September, the gathering makes me feel like we're solidly into the month. It's always worth the eight hour drive after school on Friday night. Planned by volunteers Tim Abbott and Dennis Higham, and hosted by the museum, the gathering has grown to about 125 rodmakers; there's always something new to learn, something known to share.

This year Mike Canazon adapted the casting challenge to a more integrated part of the weekend. The idea is that some of the rodmakers enter new designs, or new takes on old designs, and the best casters give them a competitive workout. Historically, many of the rodmakers were competition casters, especially the H. L. Leonard extended family whose heritage touches both Maine and Central Valley, New York, not far from the gathering. While the casting proceeded, David, Ron Barch, Dennis Higham, and others who had jointly made this year's gathering donation rod worked through a series of progressive demonstrations which mirrored their successive steps. The rod was a George Barnes "Don Taylor" taper, and David had spliced the nodeless pieces into strips, so he demonstrated that step. I was talking books with

Rolf Baginski, from Germany, and Bill Harms and
Tom Whittle, who'd published a striking volume
about Vince Marinaro that featured Kim Mellema's
incomparable artwork. Kim and I were longtime
friends reunited, and artist Michael Simon joined
the conversation, up from Virginia. Yukihiro, a
friend from Japan, explained his use of madake
cane. Jack Leary, a new maker from our class, had
afterwards volunteered to wire the museum's new
rod shop, and came back for its premier.

One of my favorite moments came just after
Walt Carpenter, a veteran of the H. L. Leonard
shop, joined the first working demonstration of
the old Halstead mill in the museum shop. When
Walt made his way over to the pavilion for lunch,
he nearly ran into ninety-year-old rodmaker Gus
Nevros who'd ridden from Ohio with Ron Barch.

"Gussy!" Walt shouted in surprise, "I thought
you were dead!"

Gus raised both arms, "Booooo!" Then he
added, "Not yet!"

September 19th, Friday

I'm rekindling the middle school fly fishing group. Its phoenix found a home on Friday's STAT period, Student Teacher Access Time, a rethinking of the old study hall plus lunch. I might not have taken it on, but some of the students from the field trip Mike and I had arranged to the Atlantic salmon hatcheries have been asking, and they've been polite and persistent. Not all of them are known by those traits. My reasoning is that if they are that interested, there's really no choice. Some things are as simple as that.

Since my principal wanted to account for the kids and give their other teachers some advanced notice, I ran a week of advanced sign-ups so I could issue both a list for the staff and library passes for the students. As soon as I e-mailed the teachers, one e-mailed me back, saying three of the students needed to be with her for missed work. Before I could reply, she immediately e-mailed again to say that she'd changed her mind: an hour with the club would probably be more productive for them in the long run. I could hear the sigh.

To make it their club rather than mine, I held a preliminary meeting to see what they'd like to learn. I was completely honest with them; the budget wasn't going to be there for any field trips

like last year or for any fishing trips. They burst
into chatter about how great the Atlantic salmon
trip had been, but they understood and wondered
if we could walk to the Kids' Pond to fish. I
explained that we could but worked in that no one
would go or attend any Friday STAT club meeting
if there was a question in my mind about his or her
behavior. Best to get that out of the way. Be good
or be gone, I smiled; that was my one condition,
and they agreed to it.

It was a little harder for them to come up with
the things they wanted to learn. Sometimes we're
all unaware of what we already know, so it takes
a moment to organize that before moving on to
what comes next, what we don't know. I started
a list on the whiteboard, just the heading, and
waited. Contemplation. They were quiet until one
asked if we could talk about which flies to choose
before you left home.

"Yeah, how do you know that?" another
student asked.

"How do you know where the fish are going to
be?" someone added.

Then hands started going up, and I wrote
as I interpreted from what they said, tying flies
to casting techniques to reading the lake depth
charts to what it takes to be a game warden. We

started sharing stories from summer, and I mined more ideas for the list from those. I included 'how to unhook a sea gull, loon, or frog.' One usually invisible boy I knew from last year raised his hand and asked how to unhook a brook trout without hurting it and looked so concerned that I didn't press for the story behind the question. Time enough for that and more when we actually get going. I did ask how many of them owned fly rods and reels since I only had eight in the library for them to share. Seven out of twenty-four kids. Hmm. I may know some people who might help with that. Equipment may get older, but there's no such thing as useless fly fishing gear.

<u>September 30th, Tuesday</u>

September may be the back-to-school month, but most schools here start in August, so September is really the recap month. It's the month to take stock of all the lessons which have come before and find the new starting point for the fresh knowledge of the following months. What was elusive is now ingrained, and the year stretching out ahead benefits from the foundation. In our district, September ends with a major cumulative test. Then we move on.

I suppose that mirrors most things in life. By September, we can look back and see that we know what we are doing, a lot of the hardest part is over, and we're invigorated by the September air, vital and alive, with the solid foundation giving us confidence to adventure on. The commonality between learning and adventure is the search; both lead to a richer, fuller life.

In angling, September 30th means that the biggest brook trout might be headed out of the lakes upstream into the remote headwaters.

The weekend, though, fell on the 27th and 28th, only a couple days off, but with the sudden heat and lack of rain after a cool, wet summer, we tested a couple streams and conditions just weren't right. Then, on Monday the 29th, the temperature dropped twenty degrees. Rain continued steadily into the evening, though not enough to bring down the last colors of the birch and maple in the clearing, leaves brilliant with the dampness. The firs and spruce looked exceptionally vivid though the window, too, shades of dark, shining greens. It was impossible to ignore the call: boughs cradling fallen leaves, deep greens spotted with yellows and reds, a blaze of orange, moody clouds hiding glimpses of a pure, autumn blue sky. Brook trout forest.

"Feel a cold coming on?" David teased me. I did, in fact. He'd seen me sneezing, and I just taken something for it. Students are germy in the fall.

"I do," I replied. "You?" In my school, we're under strict instructions. If you're sick, don't come to school. They don't say anything about having to stay home.

That we remembered the way to September 30th Pool was somewhat remarkable. We'd been there twice. The first time our guide friend had taken us there on his day off, and we were sworn to secrecy. I hadn't caught a thing. The second time was playing out the same way, cold and fishless but wild and beautiful, and I'd resolved to be at peace with the boreal beauty of the remote place when I'd finally hooked a small, autumn brook trout, a fine ending to the season until it was attacked by the Great White Shark of the North Woods. The image of that marauder stayed with us both last year when we couldn't find a way to fish here.

Then there was Labrador, like a immersion graduate class in fishing for big brook trout. The stars of that week had been the split cane rods we had made together, Dickerson 8014 Guide tapers, the Twins. They were in our hands today.

After we had returned from the Three Rivers Lodge, we discussed which efforts we'd support with the sale of one of the Twins. There was no rush; we'd pretty much decided to wait until winter or spring, then donate half to the Maine Penobscot Project for the restoration of Atlantic salmon and half to the large woody debris efforts to stabilize the sands of the Au Sable River system in Michigan. Robin's name would go along with ours. While we hadn't advertised the rod, Hutch and I had talked about it after a high school fly fishing club meeting. He didn't say a word about wanting it, but his brother told us later that he'd been carrying his checkbook to school just in case I ever mentioned passing it on. We'd be pleased for him to have it.

I balanced finding my way along the braided moose paths through the spruce and fir to the river with deciding which fly to try. In my vest were two traditional featherwing streamers, each about four inches long on a 2X hook, barbless. Made by a local tyer called Gray Wolf, they'd been a treasured gift. I knew he wouldn't mind that I'd finally arrived at putting them to good use. I chose the Water Witch, very trouty, and saved the Midnight Ghost for my last fly. David thought he'd try a different traditional approach, a Woods Special.

The water was high all right. Cold, too. 54 degrees and clear, although the dark, deep bottom gave the illusion that it wasn't. I worked my way through the alder branches at the foot of the pool, and David stepped into the water midway down. Coarse, gravelly sand under the brush allowed maybe three feet of wadable water before the black abyss. Roll casting time. The Twins were good at it by now.

David immediately caught an 8-inch brightly colored brook trout. I just felt a tug on the tail of my streamer. He caught another, equally striking, the fish of fall. I stuck to my plan, big fish or nothing. Pursuit of the elusive. By his third, he was ready to move on, to explore downstream. We swapped places, and I rolled the Water Witch out past a sheltering rock across the pool, let it sink, and stripped it in. Something chased it. The Big Fish? I cast again, stripped again, and watched more intently. Nothing. I tried again, and had just decided to move to the head of the pool when something attacked my fly. I felt a little weight, then nothing. Something small grabbing the tail again? I still had the fly, but the pool and I were both feeling cold. I offered David the spot back.

"Catch that fish," I wished him, "I'm going upstream to the little rapids."

I'd managed to negotiate the alders in some heavier current with my wading staff in one hand, Twin in the other, approaching the small line of rocks when David, behind me, saw the Big Fish flash. He yelled something, a lot of things; I couldn't hear over the water, but it wasn't necessary. I got the point. A flash was all he got, but it was impressive. He was casting again when I lost the Water Witch in the rocks.

Three hours later, I was seriously fishless and headed downstream again. David was reeling in.

"Enough," he said, contented. "I'm getting cold and my arm is sore." Translated, this meant I'm happy to smoke a cigar on the bank and bring the season to a close. He was cradling his Twin and pulling the cigar tube out of his vest as I splashed back through the alders with my Twin, then let the waters calm as I tied on the Midnight Ghost.

A peace settled over us with the twilight. Together, an exciting place, him with a good cigar, me with a fly rod that had become a friend. I loved how it would cast- reading my thoughts, forgiving my mistakes. I watched the line become a thing in itself, rolling out across the large part of the pool, then up to the foot of the rapids, then down to the final run out, and, of course, across to the sheltering rock. I cast it easily everywhere, then stripped it in again through the Big Fish's pool. He was probably long gone from all the commotion, but it didn't matter any more.

I was starting to shiver, though. Even joy couldn't keep away the chill forever. The ending feeling finally came. Standing in a wild river near the Canadian border in the remote North Maine Woods, shivering, can't be the best for a cold, but it had been a good day.

One last cast, and I wiggled the fly as it came under the edge of some alders. Something managed to grab it and hang on, an ambitious eight-inch brook trout in full color, a perfect ending fish. He disappeared the second I released him. David rose to net it, but I'd already slipped out the barbless fly and signaled him just one more one-last-cast. I rolled the Midnight Ghost out near the sheltering rock, let it sink, and stripped it part way back. It was about a rod length away when the Big Fish attacked the fly and ran.

"The Big Fish!" I sang out. "Big Fish!"

David appeared upstream with the net. My rod was arched but the Big Fish was being good to me. It was determined, but not defiant. I silently negotiated the deal, drawing upon two years of patience and lessons learned, and then turned him toward David, who gracefully scooped him in, tail first. I stood stunned as David slipped the fly free, his cigar floating beside the rim of the net. David was smiling.

Kathy Scott

About the Author

*T*om Helgeson once wrote, "Everyone who knows her or reads her books knows that Kathy Scott is a restless spirit. Her life is a manuscript evolving, chapter by chapter, episode by beguiling episode."

Kathy Scott's first book, *Moose in the Water Bamboo on the Bench,* has become a classic among those who treasure split bamboo. She was nominated for the prestigious Rutstrum Wilderness Author's Award for her second book, *Headwaters Fall as Snow.* Of her third book, *Changing Planes,* Seth Norman wrote in Fly Rod and Reel, "If you're anything like me, you'll wonder how the hell such a gentle world survives anywhere near your own continent, this place and time where a rod made by your hands is just a brilliant stop on a journey well-traveled." Her writing also appears in The Planing Form, Powerfibers, Midwest Fly Fishing, Fly Rod and Reel, and other magazines.

In 2009, Kathy Scott was recognized by the National Board of Trout Unlimited with their Youth Leadership Award for her continued work integrating fly fishing and conservation into schools.

Kathy Scott and David VanBurgel continue to pursue a life well-lived at the edge of Maine's Great North Woods, championing cold waters and their inhabitants, and romping with Effie and Midge. They've returned to magic that is Labrador, where wild, native brook trout still lord over majestic waters and respond to blue winged olives. Kathy has the flamed culms of cane ready to make her next bamboo fly rod.